UCHICAGO Consortium on School Research

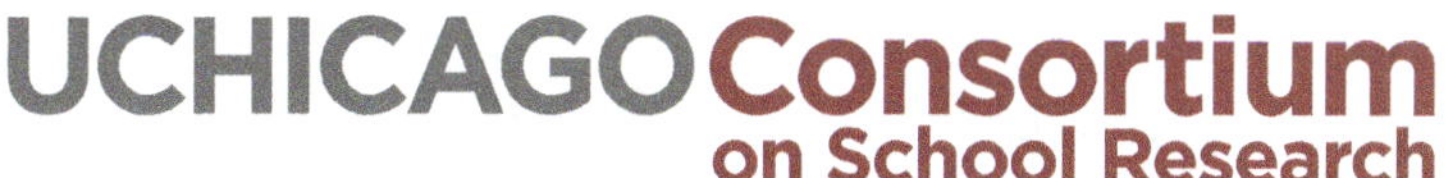

RESEARCH REPORT JUNE 2024

Mitigating the Academic Impacts of Proximity to Homicide

The Role of Schools

David W. Johnson, Rebecca Hinze-Pifer, David Orta, and Samantha Guz

TABLE OF CONTENTS

ACKNOWLEDGEMENTS

The authors would like to thank staff from Chicago Public Schools (CPS), in particular Dr. Cynthia Treadwell, Megan Hougard, Jadine Chou, Benjamin McKay, and Sarah Dickson, for their partnership and willingness to share historical and policy context and data. Dr. Maurice Swinney and the staff of the CPS Office of Equity were also instrumental in shaping and supporting the developing of this work. This report would not have been possible without the close collaboration, thought partnership, and tireless work of the late Hellen Antonopoulos.

This report benefitted from excellent research support provided by Alyssa Blanchard, whose efforts included managing and constructing analytic files for this study. Her meticulous efforts to identify appropriate survey measures and analyze their underlying factor structure greatly contributed to the development of this report. Andrew Zou, Kelsey Berryman, and Ebony Hinton provided additional support for data collection, data management, and analysis at various points along the way as well. W. David Stevens, Jessica Puller, Chen An, Elaine Allensworth, Jenny Nagaoka, Camille Farrington, and Holly Hart also provided critically important feedback and support in developing and revising drafts. The UChicago Consortium Steering Committee provided vital feedback as well, including key support from Amanda Lewis and Kafi Moragne-Patterson. Eliza Moeller with the Network for College Success also provided important feedback on early drafts, particularly on the development of qualitative findings from this report.

This development of this project was also supported at multiple points by colleagues and partners across the city. Dean Deborah Gorman-Smith and staff at the Chicago Center for Youth Violence Prevention—including Franklin Cosey-Gay—provided key feedback during the project's development. Lynn Cherkasky-Davis, Walter Taylor, and Michael Meyer at the Chicago Teacher Union Quest Center also provided key input in early stages of the work. The development of this research project and the production of this report would not have been possible without the ongoing support of the members of project's community advisory board, including Mashana Smith, Adam Alonzo, LaTonya Hill, Natalie Neris, Todd Barnett, Jacqueline Herrera, and Cathy Paliga.

Finally, the project would not have been possible without the generous financial support and thought partnership of our partners at the Joyce Foundation, the Lloyd A. Fry Foundation, the Steans Family Foundation, and Crown Family Philanthropies.

The Consortium gratefully acknowledges the Consortium Investor Council that funds critical work at the Consortium: putting the research to work, refreshing the data archive, seeding new studies, and replicating previous studies. Members include: Brinson Foundation, CME Group Foundation, Crown Family Philanthropies, Lloyd A. Fry Foundation, Joyce Foundation, Lewis-Sebring Family Foundation, Mayer & Morris Kaplan Family Foundation, Robert R. McCormick Foundation, McDougal Family Foundation, Polk Bros. Foundation, Spencer Foundation, Steans Family Foundation, Square One Foundation, The Chicago Public Education Fund, the Vivo Foundation, and two anonymous foundations. The UChicago Consortium thanks the Lewis-Sebring Family Foundation, whose operating grant supports our work.

Cite as: Johnson, D.W., Hinze-Pifer, R., Orta, D., & Guz, S. (2024). *Mitigating the academic impacts of proximity to homicide: The role of schools.* Chicago, IL: University of Chicago Consortium on School Research.

This report was produced by the UChicago Consortium's publications and communications staff: Jessica Tansey, Managing Director of Research Communications; and Jessica Puller, Senior Communications Strategist.

Graphic Design: Jeff Hall Design
Photography: iStock by Getty Images
Editing: Jessica Tansey and Jessica Puller

06.2024/PDF/jh.design@rcn.com

Executive Summary

Community violence can have traumatic effects on young people, presenting daunting challenges for families and school educators working to support students' growth, development, and achievement in school. It is critical to understand its effects on students and consider what schools can do to mitigate those effects, while working to reduce the prevalence of homicide and gun violence in the broader society.

This mixed methods study asked:

1. What is **the extent, distribution, and impact** of living in close geographical proximity to violence* on CPS students' performance in schools?
   - How do proximity to violence and its impacts on young people vary geographically and for particular groups of students, specifically students of color and those living in communities with high levels of poverty?
2. To what extent is there **evidence whether schools can insulate or protect students from the negative effects** on academic and behavioral outcomes of living in close proximity to violence, so as to support students' health and wellness?
3. What **elements of school climate and organization** are characteristic of schools that appear to protect students against the negative impacts of proximity to violence on academic and behavioral outcomes?
4. How do **adults working in schools** that mitigate the impact of living in close proximity to violence understand and describe their work?

*This study specifically looked at the effects of homicide because reports of homicide are least affected by reporting bias, and homicide rates are highly correlated with other forms of community violence.

Key Findings

- **The experience of living in close geographical proximity to homicide varied considerably for students across Chicago.**
  - Between 2011 and 2019, on average, one in five CPS students lived within 0.2 miles—roughly two city blocks—of the location of a homicide in any given year. Six percent of students had this experience multiple times in a single year.
  - Students living in Chicago's lowest income neighborhoods were the most likely to live in proximity to homicide.
  - Black students were more likely to live in proximity to homicide than their peers—but at the same time, many schools that served predominantly Black students had relatively low levels of student proximity to homicide.
- **Living in close geographical proximity to homicide negatively affected students' academic performance.** Students who lived in close proximity to homicide had, on average, lower attendance rates, lower standardized test scores, reduced GPA, and a greater likelihood of having a reported behavioral infraction, suspension, or expulsion following a homicide in their neighborhood, compared to before the homicide occurred.

- While the average effects of living in close proximity to homicide appeared relatively small overall, they likely combine cases where **a)** students are unaffected with **b)** students most directly connected to such events grapple with much larger challenges.

- Some schools mitigated typical negative effects of living in proximity to homicide on academic performance. When comparing schools serving similar students with similar experiences outside of schools, most student outcomes declined after homicide near their home—but not all schools saw average declines in student outcomes.

- Schools that mitigate the negative effects of living in close geographic proximity to homicide on students' academic outcomes were characterized by strong, positive school climates across a range of measures, including engaging instruction and trusting, connected relationships among students and between students and adults.

- Systems, structures, and routines that coordinate the support adults provide, center students, and emphasize connection and relationship between adults and young people were vital tools for the educators, administrators, and school staff interviewed.
    - Teams in schools that mitigated the negative effects of homicide faced substantial challenges—the scale of needs appeared to outpace the capacity to respond; the challenges of balancing providing direct services to students with coordinating care, particularly the burdens of data analysis and paperwork were often overwhelming; and the complexity of coordinating efforts to leverage external community resources and partnerships was considerable.

Considerations

This report offers evidence that schools can, and do, mitigate the negative impacts of adversity that young people experience. At the same time, this is complex, resource-intensive, and emotionally-taxing work, requiring time, resources and intentional strategies.

Elected, civic, and community leaders can consider:

- Greater public investment in addressing the epidemic of gun violence and the broader, longstanding historical disinvestment in communities of color throughout the city is needed for more educational equity. The degree to which students, families, and communities of color live in proximity to homicide is neither incidental nor random. Patterns of violence in Chicago, as elsewhere, are closely related to longstanding, intentionally racialized policies of social and economic isolation and neglect that concentrate poverty and hardship in communities of color over decades. This report documents the disproportionate negative impact that proximity to homicide has on the academic outcomes of students of color. It also provides evidence that educators and schools can play critical roles in mitigating some of those effects. These efforts alone will not be enough, and educators cannot be solely responsible for addressing, or more importantly preventing, violence across the city.

- Intentional, coordinated, and sustained efforts of dedicated adults in schools can address harm to students and promote their resilience. As long as there are high rates of violence in the communities that schools serve, the impact will be felt by students and families, and will require school staff to develop strategies to support students in intentional ways. Schools in communities with more violent events will require more intentional efforts and supports. Schools can play a crucial role in the lives of students who experience adversity in their lives outside school. Well-organized systems and structures, such as behavioral health teams (BHTs) and effective use of tiered, evidence-based intervention strategies can help ensure that information, resources, and support are shared in timely and responsive fashion. These structures help adults manage the complexity of providing the considerable support required to meet the needs of young people and their families. In the relatively small number of schools that face the greatest volume and most acute student needs, these systems and structures can also help to coordinate the considerably greater resources and support required.

- **Deep, sustained effort in building and sustaining strong, collaborative, and trusting relationships among adults in schools can help make schools more responsive and more effective at mitigating the negative impact of violence.** School leaders play a critically important role in helping create and sustain school communities that are responsive to students' needs. The work of building responsive school climate, however, is also broadly shared and reflects the importance of prioritizing resources and supports for creating school and classroom environments that are organized to be student-centered. Interviews with staff in schools that were more successful in mitigating the impact of homicide on students' academic performance highlighted the importance of communication, coordination, and trust across members of the school community in their efforts to support students.
- **Strong, supportive, and trusting relationships between educators and students are a crucial resource for protecting students from harm and promoting resilient school communities.** The quality of the school climate and culture matter, broadly; however, the particular quality of relationships, particularly between educators and students, is a critically important barometer for the success of efforts to mitigate the negative impacts of living in close proximity to homicide. Efforts to make school systems and structures—particularly how a school responds to student misconduct—broadly restorative are an important part of the broader strategy of focusing on relationship and connectedness.

Responsive, resilient school communities do not emerge from a single initiative, require substantial resources, and demand sustained and hard work in the face of immensely difficult circumstances. It is not the presence (nor the absence) of one or another initiative or approach to supporting students that makes a school responsive or resilient. Instead, as the findings from this report underscore, it is the interlocking of multiple different efforts intended to center and respond to the experiences, perspectives, and needs of students that create a holistic, shared approach to making schools more responsive to their needs. Partnerships between schools and community-based organizations can help to extend the reach and impact of schools' efforts as well. The development of responsive, resilient school communities is shared work and cannot be accomplished in isolation.

Introduction

Research, policy, and practice have increasingly converged in viewing public schools as critically important spaces that can and should foster not only academic achievement, but also the social-emotional growth, development, and wellbeing of young people. This perspective reflects a growing recognition of young people's wellness as both intrinsically valuable and instrumental to their academic success. At the same time, educators, policymakers, and researchers are broadening the purpose and role of schools beyond merely "identifying exceptional natural talent," to intentionally nurturing the intellectual ability of all students while recognizing their humanity and fostering their agency.[1] If educators aspire to foster students' holistic development—including their academic achievement, mental health, and wellness—they need to address the impact of violence in young people's lives.

Students, families, and communities across Chicago are affected by gun violence, but the levels and experiences differ greatly by location and by the racial composition of communities. In Chicago, recent rates of violence rose sharply during the COVID-19 pandemic, and then declined to pre-pandemic levels in 2022. Still, there were more than 4,000 gun-related injuries reported to the Chicago Police Department in 2020 and in 2021, and homicides in the city rose in tandem.[2] While overall rates of violence have fallen from peaks in the late 1990s[3] in predominantly White and Latinx communities, rates of violence in Chicago's predominantly Black communities have exceeded 1990s levels in recent years.[4] Of the 725 homicides reported in Chicago in 2022, 541 victims were Black, more than 18 times as many as were White. Proximity to violence and homicide remain profoundly racialized in Chicago.[5]

Without intentional efforts and sufficient resources, community violence will exacerbate educational inequality. The more that students and families are struggling with trauma and concerns about safety, the more it is expected of school staff to provide a nurturing environment that also fills students' academic needs. School personnel need evidence about which supports are effective, and the resources needed for those supports, so they can meet this expanded role.

Holistic health & wellness

The connection between students' holistic health and community violence is much-discussed in schools, albeit in different ways and with different resources, depending on how schools and communities are situated. Previous research has described schools both as sites where violence may occur and/or be prevented, as well as spaces that can support the healing, growth, and agency of young people and adults.[6] Chicago Public Schools (CPS) students have repeatedly advocated for expanded school-based mental health services and supports.[7] Student activists have also repeatedly called for broader policy changes, such as placing stricter restrictions on schools' use of punitive, exclusionary discipline and increasing transparency in school governance, to make schools more welcoming and inclusive places.[8] And district officials and educators have lately focused not only on teaching and learning, but have increasingly come to view students' academic performance as interconnected with their socio-emotional development, mental health, and wellness.[9]

1 Jackson, Porter, Easton, Blanchard, & Kiguel (2020); Porter, Jackson, Kiguel, & Easton (2023).
2 City of Chicago (n.d.); Rowlands & Love (2022, April 21).
3 City of Chicago (n.d.).
4 Ludwig (2023, March 27).
5 Andriesen (2023, October 12).
6 Ginwright (2010); Ginwright (2015); Osher, Guarino, Jones, & Schanfield (2021); Sartain et al. (2015); Steinberg, Allensworth, & Johnson (2011).
7 Dombo & Sabatino (2019); Thomas, Crosby, & Vanderhaar (2019).
8 Boyle (2020, July 12); Turner (2021, September 3); Walker Burke (2021, May 14).
9 Moon, Williford, & Mendenhall (2017); Nygaard, Ormiston, Heck, Apgar, & Wood (2023); Ormiston et al. (2021); Peña (2021); Peña (2022, May 10); Peña (2022, December 9); Stieber (2023, March 13).

Research questions

This mixed-methods study explores four interconnected research questions, specifically examining the particular role schools may play in the lives of students living in proximity to violence in Chicago:

1. What is the extent, distribution, and impact of living in close geographical proximity to violence on CPS students' performance in schools?
   - How does proximity to violence and its impacts on young people vary geographically and for particular groups of students, specifically students of color and those living in communities with high levels of poverty?
2. To what extent is there evidence that CPS schools can insulate or protect students from the negative consequences on academic and behavioral outcomes of living in close proximity to violence, so as to support students' health and wellness?
3. What elements of school climate and organization are characteristic of schools that appear to protect students against the negative impacts of proximity to violence on academic and behavioral outcomes?
4. How do adults working in schools that insulate students from the impact of living in close proximity to violence understand and describe their work?

Previous research on effects of proximity to violence

Many prior research studies document the negative consequences of exposure to violence on students' social-emotional development, behaviors (including academic behaviors within school and students' likelihood of being excluded from classrooms or schools for disciplinary reasons), and performance in school. Research on toxic stress in children highlights the long-run effects of unaddressed adverse childhood experiences (ACEs) on a range of both mental and physical health outcomes, including aspects of the neuroendocrine and immune systems of developing children.[10] In school-focused studies specifically looking at the effects of violence on young people, previous research links exposure to violence near home with negative changes in attention and impulse control, as well as diminished learning and academic performance, particularly on standardized achievement tests. Prior studies also link exposure to violence with negative impacts on students' engagement, school-related behaviors—including attendance—and likelihood of being suspended or expelled.[11] Negative impacts of violence on students' academic behaviors and performance also appear to vary by the age of the students, suggesting that there may be key developmental differences in how young people are affected by violence at different points in their educational careers.[12]

While existing research suggests that children and adolescents' adverse experiences—including exposure to violence and homicide in the communities where they live—have effects on their development, additional research shows that those experiences are not determinative. The long-run impacts of ACEs are determined, at least in part, by young people's access to resources and supports for making sense of and responding to these experiences.[13] Specifically, many studies have focused on the role of strong social connections to family members and peers, with particular focus on family environments and prosocial parenting styles.[14] One well-cited study, based on information gathered from 1,500 children and adolescent boys and their parents and teachers in Pittsburg public schools, examined the relationship between parent involvement and young people's behaviors, such as imbibing alcohol, smoking marijuana, unknown whereabouts, and cruel behavior toward others. The authors found that when parents

---

10 Bucci, Marques, Oh, & Harris (2016); Franke (2014); Shonkoff et al. (2012).

11 Bellis (2001); Bowen & Bowen (1999); Delancy-Black et al. (2002); Duplechain, Reigner, & Packard (2008); Gorman-Smith, Henry, & Tolan (2004); Henrich, Schwab-Stone, Fanti, Jones, & Ruchkin (2004); Matthews, Dempsey, & Overstreet (2009); Moradi, Doost, Taghavi, Yule, & Dalgleish (1999); Overstreet & Braun (1999); Sharkey (2010); Sharkey (2018); Sharkey, Tirado-Strayer, Papachristos, & Raver (2012); Sharkey, Schwartz, Ellen, & Lacoe (2014).

12 Finkelhor, Turner, Shattuck, Hamby, & Kracke (2015).

13 Huang (2014).

14 Gorman-Smith & Tolan (1998); Hardaway, Sterrett-Hong, Larkby, & Cornelius (2016); Lösel & Farrington (2012); McCabe, Clark, & Barnett (1999); Osborn (1990); Ozer, Lavi, Douglas, & Wolf (2017); Ozer & Weinstein (2004); Wyman, Cowen, Work, & Parker (1991).

had knowledge of their child's whereabouts and activities, and when children perceived their relationships with parents as positive, children and adolescents were less likely to engage in these behaviors.[15]

Prior research has also pointed to the importance of peer groups and community involvement as protective factors, suggesting that developing positive social connections outside the family can support young people's social-emotional development and wellbeing.[16] For example, a young person's perceived connection to their community was associated with protective-stabilizing effects on trauma symptomology, including internalizing (e.g., depressive, withdrawn) and externalizing (e.g., disruptive, aggressive) behaviors in youth.[17] Similarly, when young people were more likely to affirm a statement like "I feel loyal to the people in my neighborhood," they were less likely to be exposed to violence or engage in risky behaviors.[18]

Overall, research evidence on the protective role of peers and family suggests that strong social cohesion and relationships between youth and adults in schools may also play a key role to mitigate the impact of violence in students' lives. **Yet there is little research evidence on the role that schools may play in mitigating the impact of violence exposure in young people's lives.**

There is evidence that broadly links school climate to student wellbeing, including studies that find that find associations between students' perception of school climate and positive self-reported wellbeing. One such study found that when students experienced social support in school, they were buffered against the negative psychosocial outcomes—defined as emotional or behavioral problems—of youth who had been exposed to violence.[19] Similarly, a handful of studies found associations between students' sense of belonging and measures of their mental health and wellbeing, and between students' feelings of safety and overall positive academic outcomes.[20]

And while strong evidence indicates that school-based clinical or programmatic interventions can address the negative impacts of violence and other forms ACEs,[21] substantially less is known about the organizational settings those interventions are situated within, and effective school-wide approaches to effective support.

Finally, while Black and Latinx communities have advocated for cultural and structural responsiveness and for strengths-based approaches to support students' mental health and wellbeing in schools, the academic literature on school-based services to address students' mental health and wellness has largely not considered these practices in depth.[22] A recent review of the literature on trauma-informed care in schools found that the majority of research studies did not consider school context, cultural responsiveness, structural racism, or strengths-based practices.[23]

This study

This mixed-methods research study examines the role that schools may play in the lives of students living in proximity to violence in Chicago. As shared on p.9 in Chapter 1, we measure "violence" as proximity to homicide (within 0.2 miles). Proximity to homicide is an imperfect measure but is associated with other metrics of community violence. It also has the advantage of being less likely than other metrics of community violence to be biased by racialized patterns in policing and data reporting.

In the remainder of this report:

- **Chapter 1** describes the data and research methods used to address and answer the four research questions shared on p.5.
- **Chapter 2** shows that schools across the city face very different challenges in terms of the share of the students they serve who live in close geographic proximity to homicide.

15 Stouthamer-Loeber, Loeber, Farrington, Zhang, van Kammen, & Maguin (1993).
16 Li, Nussbaum, & Richards (2007).
17 Li et al. (2007).
18 Cooper (2017); Lösel & Farrington (2012).
19 Ludwig & Warren (2009).
20 O'Donnell, Schwab-Stone, & Muyeed (2002); Ozer & Weinstein (2004); Pierre, Burnside, & Gaylord-Harden (2020); Starkey, Aber, & Crossman (2019).
21 Park-Higgerson, Perumean-Chaney, Bartolucci, Grimley, & Singh (2008).
22 Thomas et al. (2019).
23 Thomas et al. (2019).

- **Chapter 3** confirms previous research that finds that, on average, living in close geographic proximity to homicide is associated with lower academic outcomes following an incident.
- **Chapter 4** shows that there are some schools in which not all outcomes decline in the wake of a homicide occurring close to where students live.
- **Chapter 5** shares the reflections of administrators, educators, and school staff in schools where multiple indicators do not decline, in order to highlight practices they feel believe make a difference for students.
- **Finally, the report concludes** with an interpretive summary that discusses the implications of these findings in the context of broader efforts to think about and support the mental health and wellness, as well as academic performance of students, particularly those living in close proximity to homicide.

The findings from this report suggest that while proximity to homicide has significant negative effects on students' outcomes, schools matter. The evidence presented herein strongly supports the notion that the choices and efforts of administrators, educators, and school staff working in concert with one another can create protective spaces for students that can mitigate the impacts of adverse experiences outside of school.

CHAPTER 1

Research Design and Rationale

This chapter describes the data, research methods, and analytical approaches used in this report in detail, including a number of key definitions and approaches to measurement that guide the analyses presented in subsequent chapters.

Data sources

This report draws on nearly a decade of administrative data about all students enrolled in CPS during the 2010–11 through 2018–19 school years, combined with publicly available data on crimes reported to the Chicago Police Department and the Cook County Medical Examiner's Office during the same time period. This includes information on 661 schools and nearly 700,000 individual students, over the course of nine school years. In each school year, there were about 300,000 students enrolled in public schools in Chicago (including charter schools), resulting in about 2.79 million student-school year observations.

The data for CPS students included home addresses at three times during the school year, as well as a variety of standard demographic and educational characteristics (e.g., free or reduced-price lunch eligibility, race, zoned school attendance, history of grade retention, special education eligibility, etc.). We constructed measures of neighborhood concentrated poverty and neighborhood social status by combining home address with data from the U.S. Census Bureau's American Communities survey.[24] In addition, in each school year we included information on individual student educational outcomes: math and English standardized test scores,[25] and grade point average (GPA) for all courses on a four-point scale. For K-8 schools, test score data were only available for grades 3-8. High school tested grades varied from year to year; we used all available data, which included scores for most ninth-graders most years, eleventh-graders since 2014, tenth-graders in some years, and rarely twelfth-graders. We also included several behavioral outcomes: percent of enrolled days the student attended school, whether the student had a recorded behavioral infraction during the school year, and whether the student was suspended during

24 Neighborhood concentrated poverty was constructed for each census block group by combining the percent of families with incomes above the poverty line and the percent of adult males who were employed. It was standardized with a high positive value, representing a high concentration of poverty. Neighborhood social status was constructed for each census block group by combining the mean educational level of adults and the percent of employed individuals working as managers or professionals.

25 Standardized test scores are the end-of-year exams given statewide each year. For grades 3-8, this was the ISAT exam through the 2013-14 school year, and the PARCC for the remainder of the study period. At the high school level, the specific tests (PARCC, EXPLORE, PLAN, PSAT, SAT) and grade levels tested varied from year to year; we included all test-grade level combinations where the test was administered to most or all students in a grade level in that year. In a few cases, tests administered in the fall were used if there was not a test administered to that cohort of students in the preceding spring. High school tests included were EXPLORE (9th) & PLAN (10th) in 2011-12 through 2013-14, PSAE/ACT (11th) in 2010-11 through 2015-16, and PSAT (9th/10th) & SAT (11th) in 2016-17 onward. All test scores were normed by year and grade level, such that the grade by year indicators in the models account for systematic differences between tests and testing years.

the year.[26] For each school in each year—including charter schools,[27] selective enrollment schools, and alternative schools—we also calculated school-year averages of each of the demographic and outcomes variables described here.

Students were not included in the sample in a given year if they did not have a reported address, had an address that could not be matched to a building in Chicago, or were enrolled for fewer than 30 days.[28] Students were removed from the sample for every year after they either moved from their first observed address or switched schools outside of a typical grade transition year.[29] The school-level analysis (described on p.12) excluded schools with fewer than 100 students in a given year, as well as schools with either fewer than 30 students who lived in proximity to homicide that year or fewer than 30 students who *did not* live in proximity to homicide that year.[30]

Data on homicide near students' homes were drawn from data provided by the Chicago Police Department that included the date and approximate location of each crime reported to police on a daily basis for the entire study period.[31] The locations in these data were accurate to the city block, but did not include the precise address. These data were supplemented by information from the Cook County Medical Examiner, which provided the precise address for homicides beginning in 2014.[32]

Measuring proximity to homicide

Characterizing what constitutes interpersonal violence is complicated. There is a wide variety of events that may be considered violent, and severity and context matter. Measuring *proximity to violence* is similarly complex: available administrative data is often missing relevant details and many violent events are never reported to police or any other social institution.[33] While much existing research on the social impacts of violence uses surveys to directly ask people what they have experienced, that approach was neither practical nor ethical with children for the large-scale scope of this study—and is known to incorporate significant error arising from imperfect recollection. Importantly in the case of young people, surveys also inadequately account for instances when children were unaware of events that produced significant changes in the behavior of adults around them, which in turn affected the children themselves.

Recognizing the complexity of conceptualizing and measuring violence and the limitations of available data, this report makes a number of intentional methodological choices in order to address the research questions. Proximity to violence was measured by combining information on students' home addresses with publicly available data on the dates and locations of crime throughout Chicago,[34] providing the number

26 These were structured as yes/no indicator variables. Suspension includes both in-school and out-of-school suspension.

27 Analysis included all available data for charter schools and their students, including addresses, attendance, and discipline data for all school years. Charter school students represented 14.8% of the student-year observations in our overall sample of 2.79 million student-years. These were are slightly more likely to be missing test scores in the early years of our study period; they represented 13.4% of students in those analyses. Analysis of student GPA never includes charter school students; our data archive currently does not include records of charter school students' course performance because of difficulty centralizing and linking these records district-wide.

28 It is not possible to determine proximity to homicide for students without a valid address. Outcomes for students enrolled less than 30 days are unlikely to reflect their time in CPS. Students who moved were dropped because including them in the sample was inconsistent with the assumptions of the model we used to estimate impacts. Schools with small enrollments were dropped because statistical estimates for small samples are imprecise and incorporate more statistical noise than useful information.

29 The impact analysis described on p.10-12 can be interpreted as a causal estimate of the impact of proximity to homicide under a certain set of assumptions. We removed students who moved because their inclusion likely violated these assumptions.

30 The "evidence of schools that were more successful at mitigating the negative effects of proximity to homicide" analysis described on p.12-13 involved creating estimates for both students who lived in proximity to homicide and who did not lived in proximity to homicide, separately for each school. We excluded schools with smaller enrollments (overall and for each group) in order to reduce statistical noise in analyses based on these estimates.

31 City of Chicago Data Portal. (2020).

32 City of Chicago Data Portal. (2020).

33 Pepper, Petrie, & Sullivan (2010).

34 City of Chicago Data Portal (2020).

of reported crimes of various types occurring within a given distance of home for each student in CPS during the course of a school year.[35]

The research team examined the prevalence of student proximity to various forms of violence, but ultimately chose to focus only on CPS students' *proximity to homicide* for two reasons. First, prior studies suggest that virtually all forms of interpersonal violence other than homicide are vastly underreported in official crime statistics[36] —and that virtually all forms of inter-personal violence recorded in official crime statistics are highly correlated with one another. Second, differential patterns of policing across communities in Chicago—and particularly in communities of color—produce skewed data that could overstate the impact of proximity to violence in communities of color and ultimately could contribute to racialized stereotypes about the lived experiences of students of color.[37]

The choice to focus on student proximity to homicide necessarily limits the implications of this report. While it is plausible—even likely—that many of the findings might be similar across other forms of violence, we are unable to provide direct evidence about how proximity to other forms of violence influences students or the extent to which schools may mitigate the effects when students experience them.

Assessing the impact of proximity to homicide

At several points, this report focuses on understanding the specific impact of living within 0.2 miles of a homicide on children's educational outcomes.[38] This focus served a specific methodological purpose—it allowed us to create school-specific estimates that have a causal interpretation under reasonable assumptions. This section explains the underlying logic of that choice.

In order to estimate the impact of living in proximity to homicide, we needed an approach that distinguished between that proximity and the impacts of many other factors that tend to be associated with neighborhood homicide. For example, there is a strong association between the extent of neighborhood poverty and prevalence of homicide. Similarly, students' risk of proximity to homicide is associated with both their race/ethnicity and their family socioeconomic status. While we can perform statistical adjustment for factors we observe, there are many unobserved factors that might simultaneously influence proximity to homicide and educational outcomes.

We addressed this problem by *comparing students to themselves in the previous year* while also adjusting for observed factors that might change over time. Models of this form are often called "value-added" models and are widely used in educational settings to account for individual-level factors that are stable between years, examining only *change* in the outcome over time. The inclusion of prior-year outcomes measures is generally understood to adjust for a wide variety of differences between students that are stable over time, but unobserved within available data.[39]

Value-added models only produce causal estimates under certain circumstances. In this case, we needed to assume that beyond proximity to homicide, there was nothing *else* systematically different for students in years of such events, compared with years when a homicide did not occur near their home. Put differently, we needed to be able to assume that the *timing* of the homicide (i.e., that it occurred for a specific student in one year rather than the next) was unrelated to other factors that might influence educational outcomes. For

35 Events were assigned to each school year beginning on the first day of summer break and extending through the last day of the school year. Distances were measured in "city block distance," rather than crows-fly distance, by adding the North-South distance to the East-West distance between two points. Because city blocks in Chicago are organized in blocks aligned to the cardinal directions, this distance is a good approximation of the walking distance between most addresses.

36 Loftin, McDowall, Curtis, & Fetzer (2015).

37 Furthermore, data from over- and under-policed communities contribute to the social construction of communities of color as violent and socially disorganized and to racial stereotypes of people of color as violent and/or threatening; we do not want to perpetuate these stereotypes. Additionally, the methods used to estimate the impacts of proximity to violence are best suited to understanding relatively infrequent but consequential events like homicide. In interpreting this report, readers should recognize homicide is just one form of violence young people encounter.

38 We used a distance of 0.2 miles because it likely reflected the proximity at which impacts were likely most acute while overcoming uncertainty in the homicide location data prior to 2014. In most parts of the city, this distance represents about two city blocks.

39 Koedel, Mihaly, & Rockoff (2015); Raudenbush (2004).

example, this assumption would be violated if a student moved, as moving changes students' risk of proximity to homicide, but also often reflects important shifts in other aspects of students' lives that may also affect their academic behaviors and outcomes. Accordingly, our analytic sample did not include students who switched addresses or schools (outside of normal school transitions like the switch that most students make between eighth and ninth grade). This accounts for scenarios like families who moved to avoid homicide, or families who moved to neighborhoods with more homicide, or families who moved because of a disruptive event like a parental job loss.

Year-to-year shifts in families' economic stability might also simultaneously influence students' risk of living in proximity to homicide and separately affect students' educational outcomes; the model below accounts for this concern, with the inclusion of indicator variables for each school-by-year and for each grade-by-year. While it is impossible to fully ensure that the required assumptions were met, it is at least plausible the impact estimates may have a causal interpretation with this combination of model and sample. These are relatively conservative assumptions and, as a result, this analysis likely underestimates the impact of geographic proximity to homicide on students' academic performance.

The basic model used to estimate the impact of proximity to homicide on students is of the form:

$$Y_{it} = \alpha_0 + \sum_{gc=1}^{4} \alpha_{gc} \cdot \text{proximity}_{it} \cdot \text{grade\_cat}_{it} + X_{it} B + Z_{i,t-1}\, \Gamma + \phi_{it} + \eta_{it} + \sum_{j=1}^{5} \alpha_j I_j \cdot \sum_{gc=1}^{4} G_{j,gc} + \varepsilon_{it}$$

In which educational outcome Y_{it} for student i in year t is predicted by:

- $proximity_{it}$: Living in proximity to homicide in year t, estimated separately by grade category (1st-2nd, 3rd-5th, 6th-8th, or 9th-12th).
- $X_{it} B$: standard demographic controls, including lunch status, race, neighborhood concentrated poverty and social status, attending zoned school, prior retention, special education status.[40]
- $Z_{i,t-1}\, \Gamma$: prior year values of all educational outcomes (i.e., math and English test scores, GPA, attendance rate, having a behavioral infraction, count of behavioral infractions, having a severe behavioral infraction, and having a suspension).[41]
- ϕ_{it} and η_{it}: groups of indicator variables for each school-by-year and grade-by-year.
- $\sum_{j=1}^{5} \alpha_j I_j \cdot \sum_{gc=1}^{4} G_{j,gc}$: a group of post-event indicators, intended to capture the notion that proximity to homicide may produce longer-term shifts in student educational trajectories.[42] The coefficients α_j represent the extent to which there is a long-term shift in student outcomes after proximity to homicide that persists throughout students' time in the district.

The coefficients of interest, α_{gc}, reflect the typical change in student outcomes in years when a homicide occurs near home, for each of the four grade categories, adjusting for all the other elements of the model. Impacts were separately estimated by grade groupings that roughly approximate developmental stages in childhood and adolescence, based on prior research suggesting the impacts of homicide manifest differently at different developmental stages.[43]

40 Missing covariates were mean-imputed and the regressions include indicators for imputation. Controls were fully interacted with the four grade categories.

41 Student-year observations were dropped from the sample if they were missing the lagged value of the Y_{it} outcome; other lagged values were mean-imputed with indicators, if missing. Lagged outcomes were fully interacted with the four grade categories.

42 Indicators "turned on" (switch from being equal to 0 to being equal to 1) permanently in the year after a given event. There are separate indicators for each event near home (1-5) at each grade category (1-4). For example, if a homicide near home occured for the first time in fifth grade, the indicator for first event in grade category 2 (3rd-5th) grade is set to 1 for each of the subsequent years the student appears in the data. In the very rare cases when students lived near more than five homicides, they were included in the analysis through the fifth event and dropped from the sample in the year of the sixth.

43 Dunn, Nishimi, Powers, & Bradley (2017); Li et al. (2022).

Using this approach, Chapter 2 reports the estimated impact by grade level category that living within 0.2 miles of a homicide had on educational outcomes for students in Chicago.[44] These estimates reflect the *average* impact of proximity to one homicide for one individual student. They do not reflect the impact of exposure to other forms of violence, the cumulative impact of proximity to homicide over time, or the impacts on students of having peers living in proximity to homicide. These estimates are lower bounds on the true impact of proximity to homicide on an average student during a year because a student's proximity to homicide might also negatively affect their peers—if, for example, a student living in proximity to homicide subsequently exhibited externalizing behavior (e.g., being aggressive or disruptive) in school that disrupted learning environments and/or created conflict with their peers. Furthermore, as prior research shows, the *typical* response to such events is often mild, but a small subset of individuals experience moderate or severe responses.[45] In that sense, estimated impacts are likely significantly smaller than what one would expect to see for the subset of individual students who are particularly troubled by proximity to a violent event.

Identifying differences across schools in mitigating the effects of proximity to homicide

In order to assess the extent to which CPS schools mitigated the negative effects of living in close geographic proximity to homicide, and specifically, to understand the ways in which proximity to homicide impacted students *differently* across schools, we used a hierarchical linear model (HLM) to produce separate estimates of the impacts of proximity to homicide for students in each school, within each grade level category, for each year.[46] These analyses were limited to high schools because the analysis described above found the impacts of proximity to homicide were concentrated at the high school level. HLM is a statistical approach designed to account for the influence of social groupings—in our case, the influence of students being grouped into schools by grade and year. The basic model is similar to the one used to estimate average impacts (described in the preceding section), in which students were observed each year they were enrolled, and these student-by-year observations were grouped together by the school that they attended each year:

$$Y_{its} = \alpha_{0ts} + \alpha_{1ts} \cdot \text{proximity}_{it} + X_{its} B_{st} + Z_{i,t\text{-}1,s}\, \Gamma +$$

$$\phi_{its} + \eta_{its} + \sum_{j=1}^{5} \alpha_{jts} I_j \cdot \sum_{gc=1}^{4} G_{j,gc} + \varepsilon_{its}$$

$$\alpha_{0ts} = \gamma_{00} + S_{ts} \Lambda_0 + \mathrm{u}_{0ts}$$

$$\alpha_{1ts} = \gamma_{10} + S_{ts} \Lambda_1 + \mathrm{u}_{1ts}$$

All other level-1 coefficients fixed across school-grade category-years

The level-1 equation is identical to the previous section, except that the estimated change in outcomes with proximity to homicide did not include a separate term for each grade-category because the level-2 units each contained students from a single grade category.

In models of this form, the level-2 random effects, u_{0ts} and u_{1ts}, capture grouping-specific values for the constant and for the change in outcome with proximity to homicide, respectively. The first is sometimes called a "school effect" and may be interpreted as the portion of student outcomes attributable to the school in that year and grade category, if the other variables in the model fully account for between-school differences in students. The second (u_{1ts}) is the value of interest. For each school-grade category-year group, it captures how *different* the typical student's outcomes were in years

44 Previous research on the relationship between students' home address and homicide has suggested that events within this distance are most consequential for students' academic outcomes. Chapter 2 provides a full discussion.

45 Bonanno & Mancini (2012).

46 The level-2 unit for this model is the school-grade category-year. For example, a school serving 3rd-8th grade students would be split into two units—one for grades 3-5 and the other for grades 6-8, with separate units for both in each year. This reflects 1) the fact that overall impact estimates were different by grade category and 2) that schools often change consequentially between years.

when a homicide occurred near a student's home. Put differently, u_{1ts} estimates the impact of proximity to homicide separately for each school-grade category-year grouping of students.

We excluded students at schools with fewer than 30 students who lived in proximity to homicide or with fewer than 30 students not in that group because the resulting estimates were statistically imprecise.[47] We conducted this analysis separately for test scores, GPA, attendance, behavioral infractions, and suspensions.

Our focus in this analysis was understanding the extent to which schools might have mitigated negative consequences of students' proximity to homicide. The largest difficulty this analysis we encountered was the concern that the types of events experienced by students at some schools may have been different than those experienced by students at other schools. To address this concern, we added controls for school-grade category-year characteristics to the level-2 equations. The S_{ts} term included school-year average values for neighborhood concentration of poverty, neighborhood social status, percent Black, percent Latinx, percent of students attending zoned school, percent previously retained, percent living in proximity to homicide, percent identified for special education services, and average values of the outcome variables.

The resulting group of estimates, u_{1ts}, reflect the school-grade category-year average difference in educational outcomes for students attending the school, after accounting for the school-specific contribution to the outcome (u_{0ts}), students' prior outcomes, and the other variables in the model. Using test scores as an example, u_{0ts} is an estimate of average student learning (as measured by test scores) at each school for the relevant year and grade category. The value of interest, u_{1ts} is an estimate of how much *different* student learning was for students at the school in years when a homicide occurred within 0.2 miles of a student's home.

When u_{1ts} is close to zero, it indicates that for that school-grade category-year, student outcomes were about the same for students experiencing proximity to homicide as they were for students who did not have that experience. When it is large, it indicates students in that school-grade category-year had large changes in educational outcomes when a homicide occurred near home.

If there is meaningful variation in these estimates—beyond what is expected due to statistical noise—it indicates that there may be meaningful differences between schools in the extent to which students' proximity to homicide translated to different educational outcomes. Our analysis did, in fact, identify some schools as more successful at mitigating the negative effects of living in close proximity to homicide on students' academic performances (see Chapter 4).[48]

Measuring characteristics of schools that mitigated the impact of violence

Differences in educators' practices might explain observed differences in schools that were able to mitigate the negative effects of living in proximity to homicide and those that were not. If so, one would expect that schools that were more supportive and responsive to students (as measured by school climate surveys) would be less likely to see student outcomes decrease in years when a homicide occurred near home.

To investigate this question, we drew on the annual *5Essentials* Survey, which is completed every spring by students in grades 4-12 and all teachers in CPS pre-K-12 classrooms, as well as other key staff members at schools. We focus Chapter 4 on findings for high schools that were more successful at mitigating the negative effects of living in close proximity to homicide because the detected impacts of proximity to homicide were concentrated at the high school level. The survey

47 The sample was already limited to schools with fewer than 100 students in a given year.

48 Statistically speaking, schools that were more successful at mitigating the negative effects of living in close proximity to homicide were defined as schools in which, on average, students' academic outcomes are not meaningfully worsened as a result of their living in close geographical proximity to homicide. For a full discussion, please see Chapter 4.

is designed to capture important elements of school climate and organization. Based on close review of the literature on protective factors associated with youth exposure to homicide, we identified 14 measures on the student survey and 11 measures on the teacher survey that prior research suggests might be protective in the aftermath of adverse experiences. Appendix A provides additional details about the survey measures and this process.

For each of these measures, we examined the statistical relationship between the measure and the school-grade category-year specific change in student outcomes with proximity to homicide (represented by $\Delta\hat{Y}_{st}$ in the equation below). Specifically, we used an ordinary least squares (OLS) regression to examine whether the estimated school-specific change in student outcomes was associated with survey-based measures of school climate and organization (M_{st} in the equation below). This approach is similar to examining a correlation but allows adjustment for the percent of students in the school who lived in proximity to homicide in that year—Exp_{st} in the equation:

$$\Delta\hat{Y}_{st} = \alpha_0 + \alpha_1 M_{st} + \alpha_2 Exp_{st} + \varepsilon_{st}$$

When the value of α_1 is positive and statistically significant, it suggests a pattern where schools which able to mitigate the negative effects of living in proximity to homicide generally had more positive measures of school climate and organization.

It is possible the observed patterns of association between the survey-based measures of school climate and the school-specific impact of homicide on educational outcomes arose from some unobserved factor that influenced both. Furthermore, readers should recognize this analysis is not capable of determining *which* measures were comparatively more important than one another in producing a supportive environment. However, the patterns observed were consistent with the notion that elements of school practice may indeed be capable of intervening in the process through which exposure to adverse events like homicide can translate into longer-run negative personal and educational consequences.

Describing educator experiences supporting students in three schools that mitigated the impact of violence

This study utilized a sequential mixed-methods design in which initial quantitative analyses were used to guide the selection of schools and collection of qualitative data. Chapter 5 in this report draws on qualitative data from interviews conducted with staff in three CPS high schools to describe the experiences and perspectives of educators and school staff in some schools that were able to mitigate the negative effects of proximity to homicide. We also spoke with staff at several community-based organizations to understand the experiences and perspectives of community-based partners who often work with educators and school staff in student support roles. Building upon Chapters 3 and 4, Chapter 5 also focuses on high schools because the detected impacts of proximity to homicide were concentrated at the high school level.

The three high schools selected for qualitative interviews were identified as schools that mitigated the typical negative impacts of living in proximity to homicide on student academic performance (e.g., GPA, standardized test scores), attendance, and disciplinary outcomes (e.g., suspensions, expulsions) via the quantitative analyses described above. **Table 1** identifies the outcomes for which each school was characterized as more successful at mitigating the negative effects of living in close proximity to homicide; see Chapter 4 for additional details. Describing the experiences and perspectives of educators in these three schools contextualizes the quantitative analyses that identified these schools as relatively more successful at mitigating the effects of living in close proximity to homicide and offers insights into how adults in those schools understood the work of supporting their students.

All three of the high schools chosen were non-selective, neighborhood high schools serving substantial proportions of students living in close geographic proximity to homicide (20-40%). One high school was located on the south side of the city, serving a predominantly Black student population. The second high school was located on the southwest side of the city, serving a

TABLE 1

Qualitative interviews were completed in 3 high schools

School	Percent of students living within 0.2 miles of a homicide, 2018-19	*Mitigated negative effects on...* GPA	Test Scores	Attendance	Behavioral Outcomes
School 1	35-40%	✔	✔		✔
School 2	25-30%	✔		✔	
School 3	20-25%	✔		✔	✔

Note: Student proximity to homicide is expressed as a range and the number of students is omitted to protect the confidentiality of participants and participating schools. Total school enrollments ranged from between 400 and 1,600 students in the three schools.

TABLE 2

Distribution of adult interviewees, by school and by role

School	Administrators	Classroom Educators	Counselors & Social Workers	Community Partners	School Staff	Total Interviews
School 1	1	1	2	4	2	10
School 2	1	6	2	–	–	9
School 3	2	6	2	–	–	10
Total	**4**	**13**	**6**	**4**	**2**	**29**

Note: Student proximity to homicide is expressed as a range and the number of students is omitted to protect the confidentiality of participants and participating schools. Total school enrollments ranged from between 400 and 1,600 students in the three schools.

predominantly Latinx student population. The third high school was located on the north side of the city, serving a mixture of Latinx and Black students.

The findings in Chapter 5 were drawn from 29 in-depth, semi-structured interviews conducted across these three high schools, including conversations with administrators, educators, counselors, social workers, community partners, and security staff. In each school, researchers began by interviewing the principal and then identified and recruited subsequent interviewees using a snowball sampling method, concluding data collection in each instance when saturation was observed.[49] Across the three schools selected, interviewees were predominantly White and female, a pattern consistent with the overall demographic breakdown of both CPS teachers and public educators in the US.[50] The demographics of the administrators, educators, and staff members in these three schools did not factor into the selection of the schools themselves and are provided here for context only. **Table 2** provides a breakdown of the adults interviewed by school and by role.

Interviews with educators, school staff, and administrators at schools that were more successful at mitigating the negative effects of proximity to homicide included a range of questions, including: protocols and processes for supporting students' mental health and wellbeing; perspectives on the climate and organization of the school community; and experiences with and approaches to building relationships with their students. In each interview, we also asked educators and staff about their own backgrounds and their experiences working at their school. In every interview, we foregrounded the aims of the study—to better understand how schools attended to the needs of students at schools where a high number of students lived in proximity to community homicide—to center this challenge in educational practice through-out the conversation. Interviews took approximately 50 minutes to complete, on average. Data were collected in-person at the first research site, and then, following the transition to remote schooling as a result of COVID-19, the remaining

49 Creswell & Clark (2017); Parker, Scott, & Geddes (2019).

50 Chicago Public Schools (n.d.b.); U.S. Department of Education (2023).

interviews at the second two sites were conducted over Zoom. Following interviews, interviewees were also provided with information about mental health resources for educators and an honorarium in the form of an electronic gift card. Following a snowball sampling recruitment method, upon completing an interview, we asked interviewees to refer us to other adults in their school whom they believed could share some insights with us about how educators were meeting the needs of their students in the adverse circumstances related to community violence.

The decision to sample only schools that mitigated the negative effects of proximity to homicide limits the ability to draw strong, definitive conclusions from the qualitative data about what differentiated protective practices or approaches. **This type of analysis is not causal**; the data collected across the three high schools discussed herein do not support claims about the distinctive presence or effectiveness of particular mindsets, practices, or interventions in schools that insulated students from the negative effects of proximity to homicide. **However, the data collected provide insight into the experiences, perspectives, and choices of adults working to support and nurture students within these schools.**

CHAPTER 2

Understanding Proximity to Homicide in Chicago and in CPS Schools

The evidence presented in this chapter shows that CPS students' proximity to homicide is strongly determined by historical and ongoing patterns of residential segregation by race and class across the city.[51]

The medical anthropologist Paul Farmer, among others, described the ways in which these complex histories of race and privilege are inscribed on young people and families as a form of what he termed structural violence—structural, because it reflects a history of intentional policy choices that often produced predictable and durable patterns of disadvantage and vulnerability; and violence, because the consequences of those choices reflect real and preventable harm done to the children, families, and communities affected.[52]

Measures of students' proximity to homicide or other forms of violent crime are, in this important sense, not measures of any characteristic of those young people, but rather a proxy for the inequities that exist in the social and structural contexts that young people and their families inhabit.

Student proximity to homicide

Between the 2010–11 and 2018–19 school years, 22% or slightly more than one in every five CPS students lived within 0.2 miles—roughly two city blocks—of a homicide in a typical year (**see Figure 1**).[53] Importantly, that means that 78% of CPS students did not experience living in close proximity to homicide in a given year.[54]

Some CPS students experienced living in close proximity to homicide multiple times in the same school year; nearly 6% of students lived in proximity to more than one event during the year. Students elsewhere in the city were unlikely to ever live in proximity to homicide. Although negative effects on students' academic outcomes persisted well beyond the 0.2-mile radius used here, we continue to define "close geographical proximity" as living within 0.2 miles or two city blocks of a homicide for clarity and consistency.[55]

51 Loury (2023, June 19).

52 Farmer (2003).

53 This report examines students' geographical proximity to homicide. As noted in the earlier discussion of data and methodology, the data on violent crime that is publicly available through the Chicago Police Department suffers from a number of important limitations. It can be simultaneously true that some types of violent crime are systematically underreported in the police department data and that other types of violent crime may be overrepresented, particularly in communities of color, where patterns of over-policing may systematically distort the information. As a data point, homicide is less likely to be affected by either of these limitations and therefore represents a more accurate measure of students' proximity to violence. Readers should note these data do not include police-involved incidents unless they are officially classified as homicide by police; in recent years Chicago police have fatally shot about 10 people each year (University of Illinois at Chicago, 2023). For a fuller discussion of the data used in this report, please see the data and methods section.

54 Data on students in temporary living situations does not reliably exist across all years included in this analysis. Students for whom no address existed in the data were removed from the analysis. Many students who were flagged as living in temporary situations did have addresses listed. In a statistical sense, this is a form of measurement error that should bias our findings toward zero impact.

FIGURE 1

Percent of Students Living near Homicide Each Year

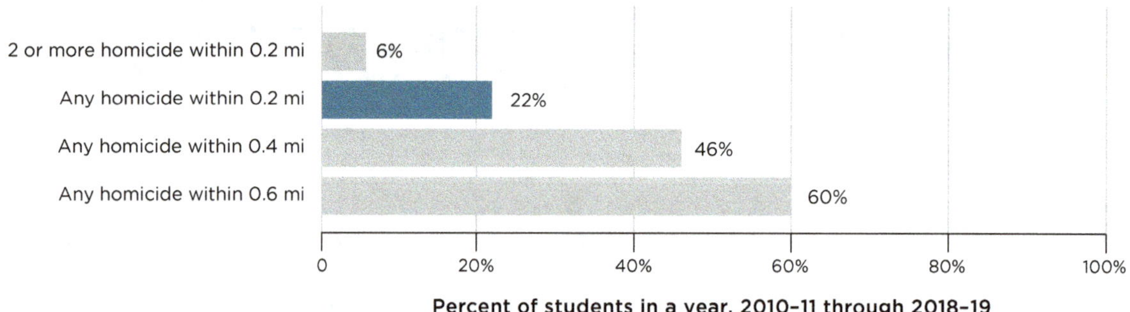

Note: Annual average between 2010-11 and 2018-19. The smallest distance—0.2 miles—is roughly two city blocks in Chicago. This is based on about 2.79 million student-year observations, or about 300,000 students each year. This reflects 97% of students in Chicago schools, including those in charter, selective enrollment, and alternative schools. The remaining students were dropped from analysis either because available data did not include an address that could be matched to any Chicago address or because they were enrolled for fewer than 30 days. Homicide includes all events classified as such in official police records. None of these include cases of police violence unless officially classified as such by police records.

Variation across communities

CPS students' proximity to homicide near home differed substantially across neighborhoods in the city, reflecting longstanding and ongoing patterns of socioeconomic and racial segregation in Chicago.[56] Although many students attend school outside their assigned attendance boundaries in Chicago, most students in these years still attended a school within a mile of home. As a result, the large differences in students' proximity to homicide across communities were ultimately reflected in vast differences across schools in the number and proportion of students whom they served, who lived in close geographic proximity to homicide.

Although high rates of homicide were concentrated on the south and west sides of the city, there was large geographical variation both across the city and between neighboring census tracts. **Figure 2** on p.19, maps the percent of students living near a homicide (showing the annual average from 2010-11 through 2018-19) by census tract, which are designed to comprise about 1,200 households each. About one-third of CPS students lived in a census tract where fewer than 10% of students live in proximity to homicide in a typical year; 8.7% of students lived in census tracts where more than one-half of students were in proximity to homicide in a typical year.

Variation across schools

Geographic patterns of variation in proximity to homicide were reflected at the school level because students tended to attend schools near home. For both K-8 schools and high schools,[57] student proximity to homicide was closely related to the concentration of poverty in students' residential neighborhoods, as shown in **Figure 3** on p.20.

Each dot represents one school, with the vertical axis showing the percent of students living in proximity to homicide and the horizontal axis arranging schools by the school average of the poverty level in students' neighborhoods.[58] The size of the dots represents the

55 Communities across the city not only experience homicide to differing extents, but also have substantially different resources that they are able to bring to bear at a community level in response. These differences across communities might, for instance, affect the magnitude of the impact of proximity to homicide from one community to the next. Statistically, these differences are addressed through the controls included in the HLM models described in Chapter 1 and in the appendices.

56 Loury (2023, June 19).

57 Chicago elementary schools typically serve students between kindergarten and eighth grade; the city has very few middle schools and very few combination schools spanning the typical school transition that occurs between grades 8 and 9. All schools with a maximum of eighth grade or below were analyzed with the K-8 group, and all schools with a minimum ninth grade or above were analyzed with the high school group. In rare cases (26 in our sample), schools included both elementary and high school grade levels. In these cases, data for schools is split into K-8 and high school grade levels, and analyzed as if they were separate schools.

58 This number and analysis included more schools than were included in the school-level analysis presented in Chapter 4. That analysis dropped relatively small schools for statistical reasons explained in Chapter 1. Analysis was performed separately for K-8 and high schools.

FIGURE 2

The likelihood of living near homicide varied considerably for students and families living in different communities across the city

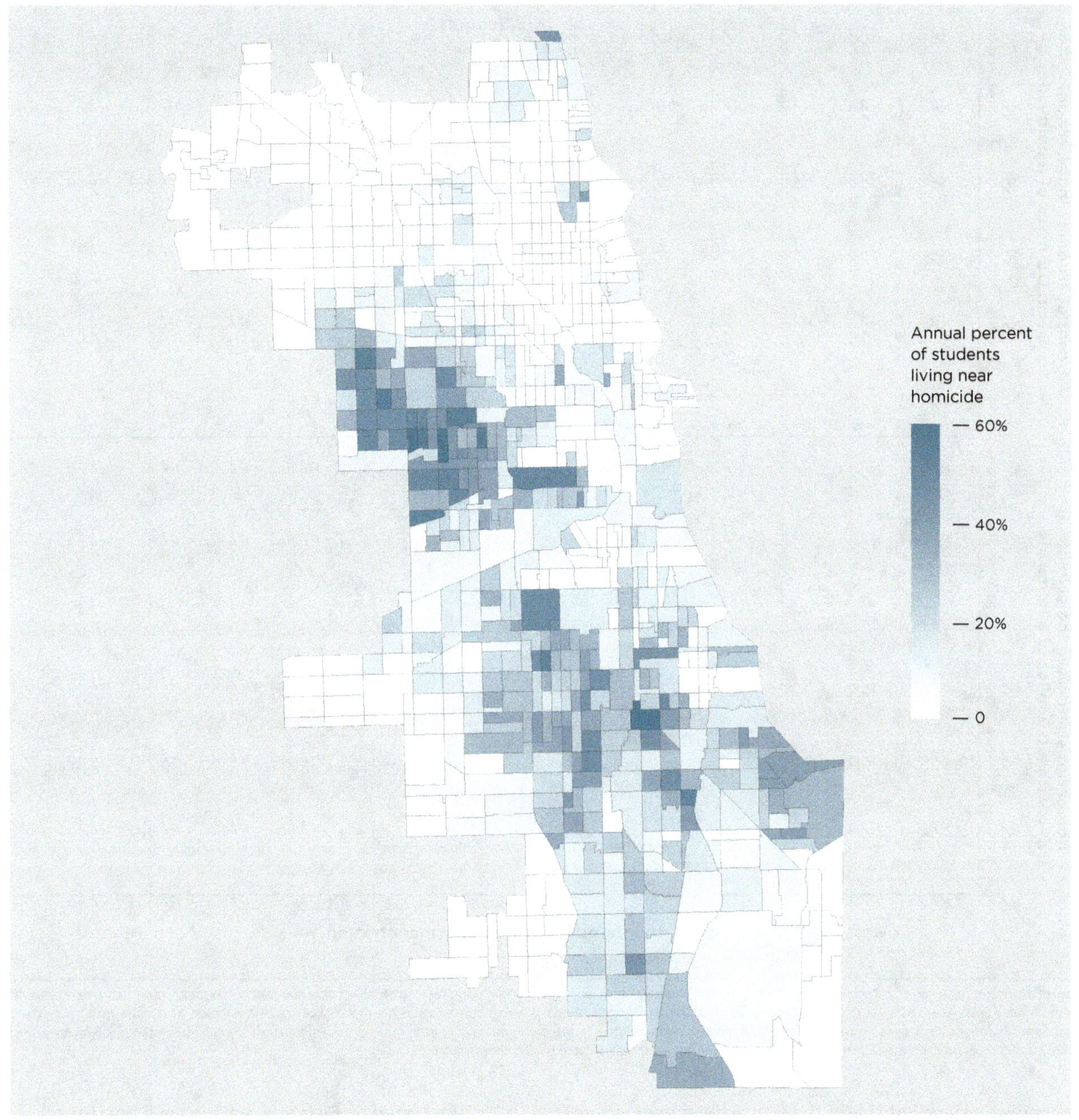

Note: Percent of students living in each census tract who experienced proximity to homicide during one year, averaged over the 2010-11 through 2018-19 school years. Proximity is defined as a homicide occurring within 0.2 miles of home.

enrollment of the school. K-8 schools had higher rates of both proximity to homicide and concentration of poverty than high schools, because CPS K-8 schools typically serve students from a smaller geographic region of the city.

For schools on the bottom of the graphs, few students lived in proximity to homicide. At the same time, students in these schools tended to live in neighborhoods where most households had sufficient income to meet their material needs. For schools on the top of the graphs, many students lived in proximity to homicide—around 80% for the highest K-8 schools and 50% for the highest high schools. At the same time, students in

FIGURE 3

Schools with higher rates of students living in proximity to homicide tended to serve communities with high concentrations of poverty

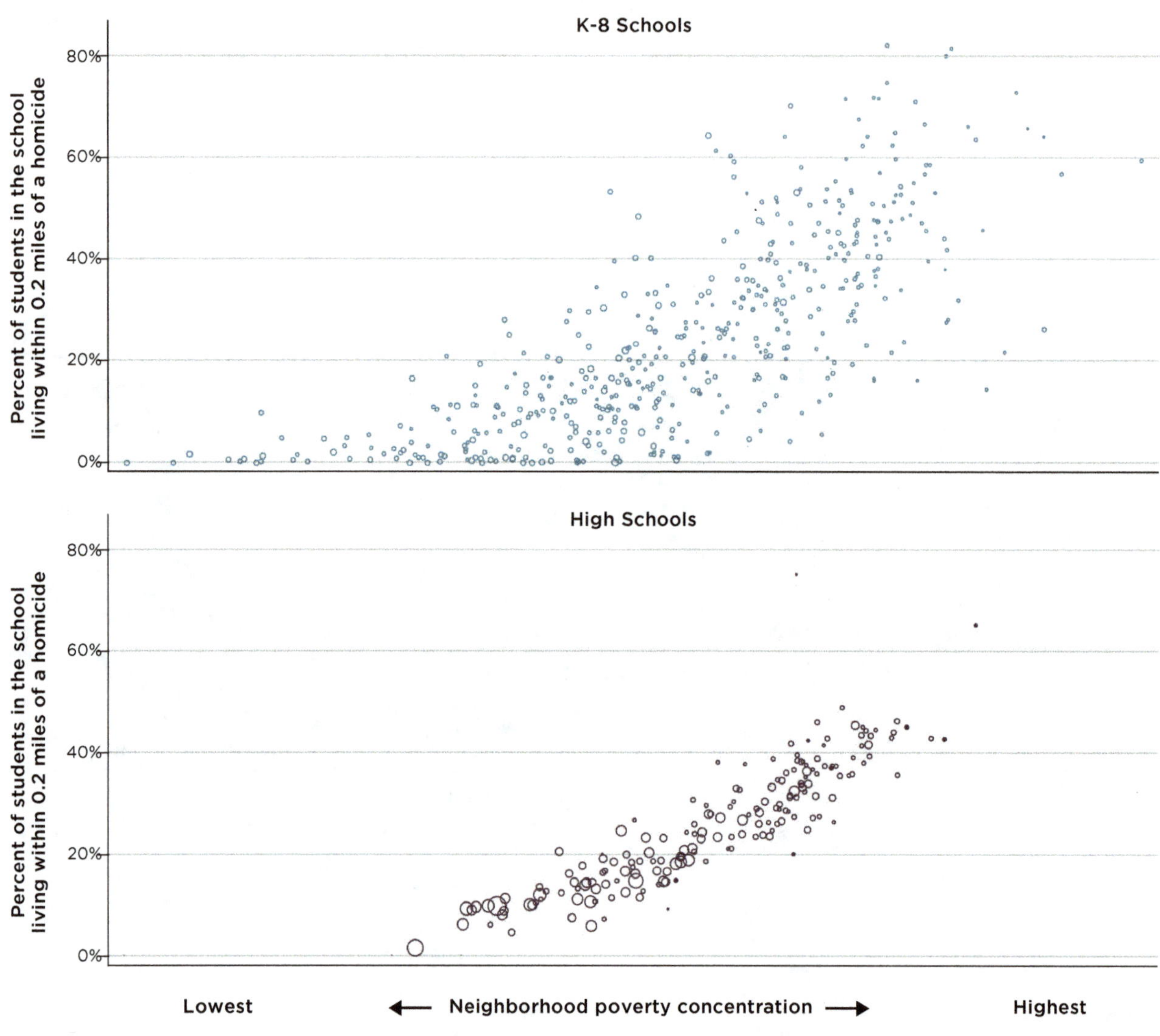

Note: Each dot represents one school in the 2018-19 school year (502 K-8 schools and 185 high schools, with 26 schools appearing in both groups). Dot size represents enrollment. Schools with fewer than 30 students are not shown. Neighborhood poverty concentration is the school-specific average of concentrated poverty in students' neighborhood, based on a combination of family income relative to the poverty line and adult male employment rates in each students' census block group. We intentionally omitted the numerical values, as the relative rankings are more readily interpretable.

schools on the right side of the figure lived in neighborhoods with the highest concentration of poverty.

To examine how history, geography, and residential segregation translated into the patterns of proximity to homicide we observe within the school system, schools were categorized based on the percentage of Black and/or Latinx students they served.[59]

As illustrated by **Figure 4**, within each horizontal box representing school racial composition category, there was large variation in students' proximity to homicide. Schools serving predominantly Black students had higher average student proximity to homicide, and accounted for most of the schools with the highest concentrations of student proximity to homicide. Historical

59 Schools were placed in these categories based on all students enrolled for more than 30 days during the 2018-19 school year and the race/ethnicity recorded in student administrative records. This approach likely obscured meaningful nuance in a number of ways, including its inability to accurately reflect the experiences of multiracial students, who were sometimes recorded within a multiracial category (which appears in our "other" group) and sometimes recorded in one category.

FIGURE 4

Student proximity to homicide was related to school racial composition, but large variation existed within each group

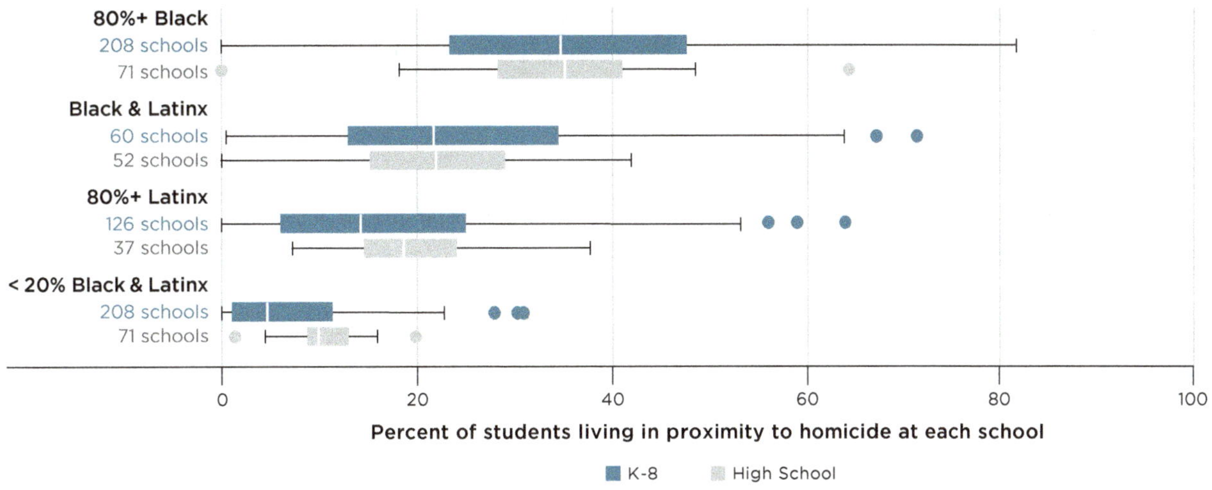

Note: Each horizontal bar shows the distribution of student proximity to homicide by school in the 2018-19 school year (502 K-8 schools and 185 high schools, with 26 schools appearing in both groups). The middle line in each horizontal box shows the percent of students living in proximity to homicide for the median school; the left and right edges of the boxes show the 25th and 75th percentiles, respectively. The dots are schools that were statistical outliers within the distribution. Schools were placed into one of four mutually exclusive groups based on the race/ethnicity of enrolled students. Schools in the "Black & Latinx" group served a student population that was more than 80% Black and Latinx students—and neither Black nor Latinx students comprised 80% of the student body.

patterns of residential segregation and systematic underinvestment in Black and Latinx communities produced heavily racialized patterns of proximity to homicide.[60] At the same time, the racial and ethnic composition of the school was not deterministic of the degree to which its students lived in proximity to homicide. Although students of color were more likely to live in close geographical proximity to homicide broadly, it was hardly a universal experience among Black and Latinx students in CPS—many schools that served predominantly Black students had relatively low levels of student proximity to homicide.

Repeated proximity to homicide

It was much less common for students to experience proximity to homicide as a repeated, ongoing, or routine event in their neighborhood.[61] Twelve percent of CPS students experienced repeated proximity to homicide—defined as more than once every year over a period of four years. In the 2018–19 school year,[62] about one-half of CPS schools—321 of the 653 schools with 30 or more enrolled students—had 10% or more of their students living in repeated proximity to homicide. Of those schools, 148 had more than 25% of students with that experience. In contrast, 116 schools mostly K-8 schools[63] —had less than 1% of their students living in repeated proximity to homicide.

In **Figure 5**, each horizontal bar represents one school, with the vertical height of the bar representing the number of students enrolled in the school. The colors reflect the frequency with which homicide occurs near students' homes. In schools at the top of the figure,

60 Loury (2023, June 19).

61 These terms do not satisfactorily encompass the circumstance we discuss here. For most things, once a year is not necessarily "routine," "ongoing," or "repeated"—but for rare and extreme events like homicide these terms capture an important aspect of the experience that is different than one-time proximity to an event. We use "repeated" here to mean at a rate of once a year or more over at least four years.

62 To avoid confusing school-by-year observations with the fact that our definition of persistent proximity to homicide was necessarily based on multiple years of data, this section reflects a snapshot of the most recent school year included in the analysis. The substantive findings are consistent for all years starting with the 2014-15 school year, and similar but at slightly lower levels in earlier years (e.g., in the 2013-14 school year 9% rather than 12% of students experienced persistent proximity to homicide, but those students were still much more likely than other students to attend schools with peers who also experienced persistent proximity to homicide).

63 It is much more typical for K-8 schools than high schools to serve such a small proportion of students experiencing repeated proximity to high school because high schools draw their students from across larger geographic areas than K-8 schools do. Only seven of the 116 such schools were high schools.

very few students experienced repeated proximity to homicide, while in those at the bottom, a sizeable proportion of students had that experience. The white lines in **Figure 5** show where 1%, 10%, 25%, and 50% of students had a homicide occur near home once per year or more. Although schools where 25% or more students experienced repeated proximity to homicide represent a relatively small share of schools in the city, they were attended by almost one-half (47%) of students experiencing repeated (once a year for four years or more) proximity to homicide.

FIGURE 5

Students who lived near repeated homicide were more likely to have classmates living near repeated homicide

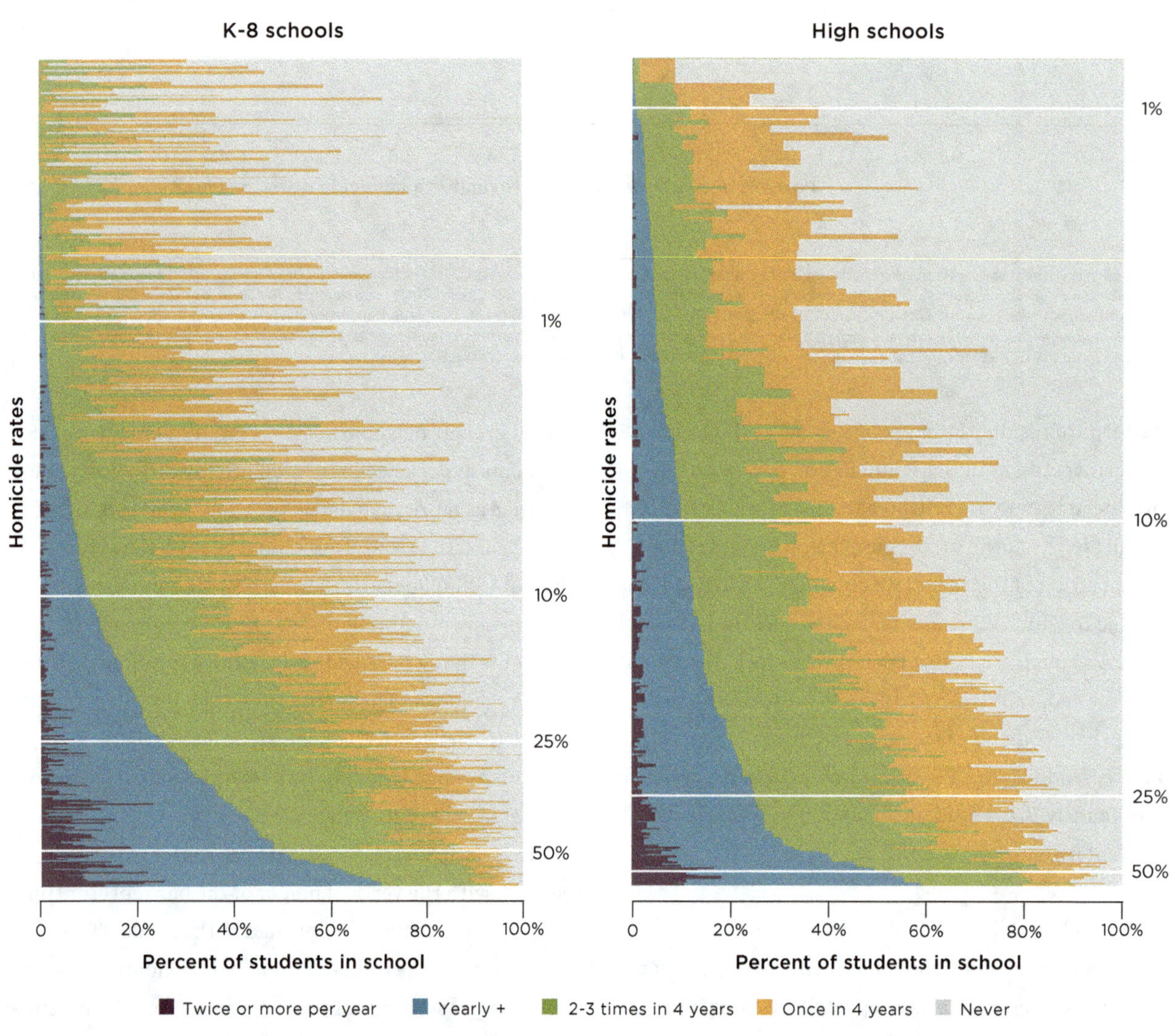

Note: Students with four years of data were sorted into groups based on the frequency of homicide near home, over the four-year period, and then organized by which school they attended. Each horizontal bar represents one school (494 K-8 schools and 184 high schools, with 25 schools appearing in both groups). Wider bars are schools with larger enrollment. Data represents the 2018-19 school year, using the 157,749 students with four years of data. Horizontal orange lines show the point at which schools had 1%, 10%, 25%, and 50% of students living near persistent homicide.

CHAPTER 3

The Impact of Proximity to Homicide on Student Outcomes

This chapter examines whether and how proximity to homicide affected CPS students' academic and behavioral outcomes district-wide. It considers variations by students' age and by different measures of students' academic performance: test scores, GPA, attendance rates, and behavioral infractions.

It can be challenging to separate out the long-run consequences of living in close proximity to homicide from many of the long-run consequences of other factors associated with it (e.g., poverty). Our analyses attempted to do this by identifying changes in each student's outcomes following a homicide, relative to their outcomes prior to the homicide. This likely results in an underestimate of the effect of proximity to homicide on student outcomes.

The findings from this study largely echo what previous research has found: CPS students' test scores, GPA, attendance rates, and likelihood of being written up or suspended for a behavioral infraction were negatively and significantly affected by living in close proximity to homicide. And there was a longer-term, cumulative persistence of negative effects of living in close proximity to homicide on standardized test scores.

Chapter 4 shows these effects differed based on the schools students attended—but first, let's look at overall, district-wide patterns.

Effects on educational outcomes: short-term

In years in which a homicide occurred within 0.2 miles of CPS students' homes, standardized test scores,[64] GPAs, and attendance all declined, while students' likelihood of being written up and/or suspended[65] for a serious behavioral infraction in school rose (**see Figure 6**). However, the impacts were meaningfully different by student grade level and outcome, perhaps reflecting developmental differences and/or differences in social networks between younger and older students. Attendance declined for students in all grade groups. Importantly, early elementary and high school students had lower learning outcomes and increased behavioral issues; they appeared to be more negatively affected than students in grades 3-8, who did not show these changes.

Some students had a homicide occur near home multiple times. When we compared the first time we observed a homicide occurring near a students' home to the second, third, or fourth time,[66] we found there was

64 Standardized test scores are the end-of-year exams given statewide each year. For grades 3-8 this was the ISAT exam through the 2013-14 school year and the PARCC for the remainder of the study period. At the high school level, the specific tests (PARCC, EXPLORE, PLAN, PSAT, SAT) and grade levels tested varied from year to year; we included all test-grade level combinations where the test was administered to most or all students in a grade level in that year. In a few cases, tests administered in the fall were used if there was not a test administered to that cohort of students in the preceding spring. All test scores were normed by year and grade level, such that the grade by year indicators in the models account for systematic differences between tests and testing years.

65 Includes both in-school and out-of-school suspensions.

66 For the subset of students who repeatedly live in proximity to homicide.

FIGURE 6

High school students' outcomes were most affected by proximity to homicide

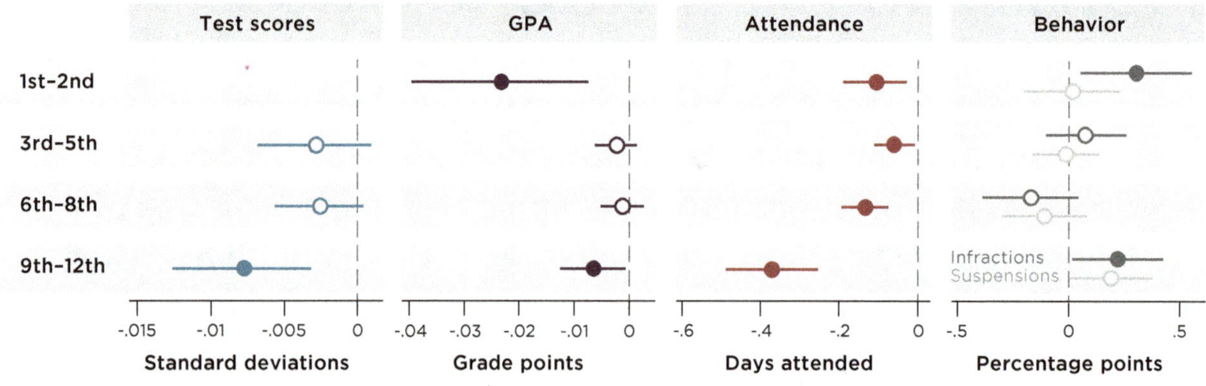

Note: Each dot represents the estimated change in student outcomes in years when a homicide occurred within 0.2 miles of home, adjusting for prior outcomes and student characteristics. Solid dots indicate estimates are statistically significant at the 5% level. Solid dots are statistically different than zero. and transparent dots are statistically equal to zero. There is no estimate for test scores in grades 1-2 because most students in those grades did not take standardized tests during the study years. Estimates were based on all students with outcomes and covariate data for each year in 2011-12 through 2018-19; data from the 2010-11 year is only used to estimate prior year information for the 2011-12 school year (as those students did not have prior year data in the data set). Test score estimates were based on about 1.32 million student-year observations. GPA estimates were based on about 1.25 million student-year observations. Attendance and behavior estimates were based on about 2.1 million student-year observations.

not a measurable difference between the shift in student outcomes for the first time vs. later times.[67] Thus, the estimated impact of proximity to homicide was the same (statistically) for the second, third, and fourth as it was for the first.[68]

The overall average effects of living in close geographical proximity to homicide on CPS students' academic performance often appeared relatively small. For high school students, on average, test scores declined by less than 1% of a standard deviation, GPAs declined by about one letter grade in one class for a student taking seven classes, students attended about one-half a day less of school, and students' risk of reported behavioral infractions and suspensions increased by about one-quarter of a percentage point.

However, the small estimates likely arose from how those effects were estimated: the observable effects were averaged across all students who were living within 0.2 miles from where a homicide occurred, including both students who were more and less directly affected. Within that radius, some young people may have been unaware that a homicide had occurred (although previous research suggests adults around them were more likely to be aware). Some subset of young people, however, may have been much more directly impacted by a homicide near home—they may have encountered the scene or the associated activities of police and first responders; they may have been personally acquainted with victim(s), family members, or friends, they may have heard about the event via social media or word of mouth.

The existing research literature suggests that this group of students is likely to experience significantly greater negative effects on their performance in school.[69] And after acute exposure to homicide, it is typical for some people to be only mildly affected, while others experience sizeable negative consequences.[70] While the measurable negative effect appears relatively small on average, were it possible to estimate the impact for

67 To conduct this analysis, we added an interaction term to the equation described in Chapter 1, which separately estimated the impact of each observed occurrence of proximity to homicide. The average impact estimate shown in Figure 6 did not change appreciably, and the interaction terms were generally not sizeable or statistically significant.

68 Prior theoretical and empirical research is somewhat contradictory, with some studies suggesting the impact of violence is smaller with repeated exposure while others suggesting consistent or even increasing with subsequent events. We found that similar impacts for subsequent events (neither increasing nor decreasing in size) in this setting.

69 Bonanno & Mancini (2012).

70 Bonanno (2004); Rutter (1985).

only those students who were somehow more directly connected to and more influenced by the event(s) in question, we would expect to see substantially larger negative effects on students' overall, including their academic performance.

Effects on educational outcomes: long-term

In addition to the short-term negative impact of a single incidence of living near a homicide on CPS students' academic performance, for the years after proximity to a homicide, student test scores were persistently lower than they were in the year prior to the event. This pattern was not present for attendance rates, GPAs, or reported behaviors.

Adjusting for the same demographic characteristics and prior outcomes as the previous approach, **Figure 7** compares students' test scores in the years before and after their first observed proximity to homicide, relative to observably similar students.[71] Each dot in the figure is the difference between the students who lived near homicide in the noted year and the group of comparison students (who lived in proximity to homicide in other years). The vertical lines are error bars; numbers within the error bars are statistically equivalent to one another. Prior to proximity to homicide, these students had statistically identical test scores to those peers (the error bars include zero). For several years afterwards, their test scores were lower than peers by a small, statistically significant amount.

Finally, every time a homicide occurred near a student's home, it had about the same impact, regardless of whether it was the first instance or the fourth (not shown). This evidence, combined with the evidence that the impact of proximity to homicide for test scores *persisted* over time, suggests that for test scores, declines were likely cumulative—with the second, third, or fourth such event further lowering student test scores. This pattern was not present for attendance rates, GPAs, or reported behaviors.

FIGURE 7

Student test scores remained lower for several years after proximity to homicide

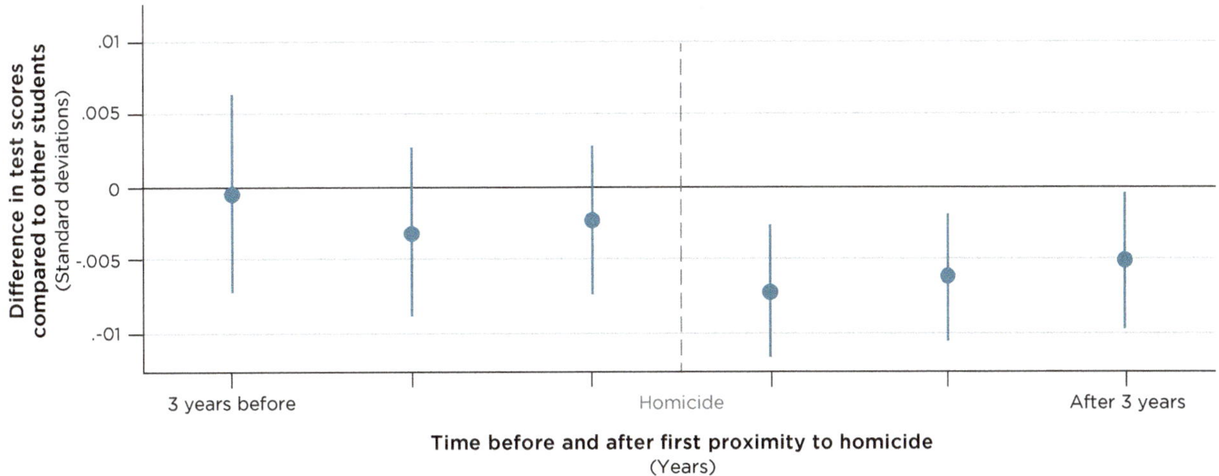

Note: Each dot represents the estimated change in student outcomes in years when a homicide occurred within 0.2 miles of home, adjusting for prior outcomes and student characteristics. Solid dots indicate estimates are statistically significant at the 5% level. Solid dots are statistically different than zero. and transparent dots are statistically equal to zero. There is no estimate for test scores in grades 1-2 because most students in those grades did not take standardized tests during the study years. Estimates were based on all students with outcomes and covariate data for each year in 2011-12 through 2018-19; data from the 2010-11 year is only used to estimate prior year information for the 2011-12 school year (as those students did not have prior year data in the data set). Test score estimates were based on about 1.32 million student-year observations. GPA estimates were based on about 1.25 million student-year observations. Attendance and behavior estimates were based on about 2.1 million student-year observations.

71 To conduct this analysis, we created a variable that indicated the number of years before or after a student's first observed proximity to homicide. We removed the year of proximity and the post-proximity indicators from the equation described in Chapter 1, replacing it with indicators for each of these years. All other control variables were included (demographic controls, prior student outcomes, and school-by-year and grade-by-year indicators). For simplicity of interpretation and statistical precision, the analysis was performed for students from all grade levels, but excluded students who did not have at least four years of data.

CHAPTER 4

Identifying High Schools that Mitigated Declines in Student Outcomes

This chapter shows there is *meaningful variation among schools* in the impact of proximity to homicide that persisted when we adjusted for differences in student characteristics. There are schools where there was no decline in students' educational outcomes, and even some schools where students had stronger educational outcomes. We also examined what teachers and students reported about their school experiences to provide some context for understanding why student outcomes might withstand the effects of violence in some schools more than others.

We limited the analysis to high schools in this chapter—Figure 8 and Table 3—because the detected impacts of proximity to homicide were concentrated at the high school level in **Figure 6 on p.24.**

The impact of proximity to homicide on student outcomes was different across high schools

There were considerable differences across schools in the degree to which their students' academic outcomes declined when there was a homicide in close proximity to their residence. To show these differences, we divided schools into three categories:[72]

1. Schools in which **student outcomes worsened** significantly following proximity to a homicide near home (e.g., attendance, GPAs, and test scores declined; the likelihood of suspensions[73] rose)—this was most typical;
2. Schools in which **no statistically significant change in student outcomes was evident** following proximity to a homicide near home. In some cases, there may have been a small decline in student outcomes, but it was statistically indistinguishable from zero; and
3. Schools in which there were **statistically significant improvements in student outcomes** following proximity to a homicide near home.

We examined school-specific estimates separately for each of the four outcomes: attendance rates, GPAs, test scores, and behavioral infractions.[74] **Appendix B** presents the full histograms of school estimates, which are summarized below in **Figure 8 on p.27.** **Appendix B** also provides similar histograms for K-8 schools for all outcomes. High schools selected for inclusion in our qualitative analysis detailed in Chapter 5 were drawn from these latter two categories, as examples of schools

72 Statistical significance for school estimates was calculated directly as part of the model estimation process.

73 Chapter 3 considered both suspensions and behavioral infractions. Here in Chapter 4, we narrowed analyses to only suspensions for simplicity; outcomes were nearly identical for suspensions and behavioral infractions.

74 We excluded schools with fewer than 100 students in the grade category or with fewer than 30 students in either the "lives in proximity to homicide" group or the "does not live in proximity to homicide" group, as discussed in Chapter 1.

FIGURE 8

In most high schools, outcomes worsened with proximity to homicide—but some schools mitigated worsening of student outcomes

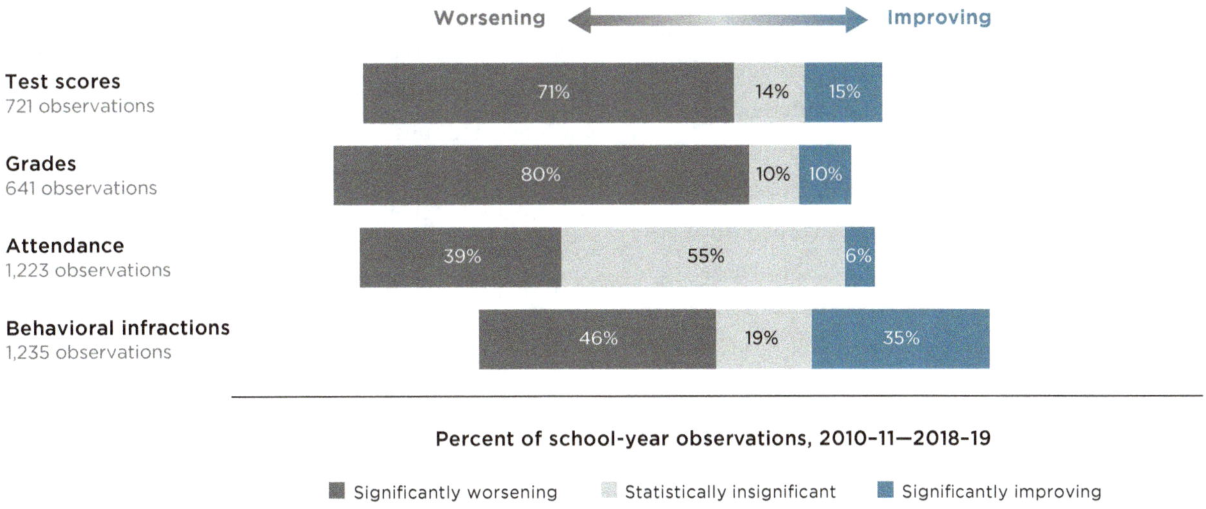

Note: Each bar shows the percent of school-year observations in which the change in student outcomes (adjusted for covariates) fell into each category. For each outcome, the stacked bars sum up to 100%. Sample size varies for each outcome due to the combination of differences in data availability for the outcome and sample restrictions described in Chapter 1.

that prevented declines in student outcomes (**also see Chapter 1, p.14** for a full description of the school sample selection).

We found that the impact of students' proximity to homicide was not the same across high schools—even when comparing schools attended by similar students—and, in some instances, schools mitigated the declines in student outcomes that usually occur. **Figure 8** shows the distribution of school-by-year specific estimates of the impact of proximity to homicide for each of four outcomes: attendance, GPAs, test scores, and behavioral infractions.

For schools on the left side of the figure, proximity to homicide corresponded with a decline in educational outcomes. For example, in 71% of high schools, test scores predictably declined with proximity to homicide—consistent with the overall estimates presented in **Chapter 3, Figure 6 on p.24**. However, in 14% there was not a statistically significant change, and in 15% test scores actually increased. Similarly, in most high schools, student attendance and GPA declined with proximity to homicide. In a subset of high schools, however, these student outcomes were unchanged or improved after students were in proximity to homicide. The behavioral infractions data shown in **Figure 8** was slightly different—on that outcome, a larger group of schools mitigated the typical increases in behavioral infractions.

Most high schools that played a protective role on one outcome did not mitigate declines across *all four* outcomes. Schools that played a protective role on GPA were more likely to play a protective role on test scores and behavioral infractions. Schools that played a protective role on attendance tended not to play a protective role on test scores, suggesting students' test scores may have been differently affected by school supports than other educational outcomes.

The school-specific estimates were relatively stable from year to year. Across outcomes, it was more common for a schools mitigated declines (or not) from one year to the next than for a school to stop (or start) playing a protective role.

Taken together, these patterns suggest three things:

1. The effect on students of living in close geographic proximity to homicide varied meaningfully across schools that served similar students;
2. A subset of schools mitigated the well-documented negative educational consequences of students living in close geographical proximity to homicide; and

3. Schools varied in their capacity to insulate students from the negative educational consequences of living in proximity to homicide.

While this analytic approach was unable to fully rule out causes of these differences arising outside of schools, the most plausible explanation is that differences in educator practice, school climate, and other within-school factors could produce these differences in student outcomes. This suggests that schools may play a protective role, meaningfully disrupting the typical negative impacts stemming from living in proximity to homicide. How educators and schools respond to the needs of students matter for whether adverse experiences outside of school translate into negative academic outcomes.

Schools that were more successful at mitigating the effects of proximity to homicide included a diverse range of schools. We compared the distribution of various school characteristics, finding that the distribution for schools that were more successful at mitigating the effects of homicide was largely overlapping for all characteristics examined and that there were no systematic patterns in which more (or less) advantaged schools were consistently placed into the protective role category. **Appendix C** provides examples.

It is possible that some schools showed little or no discernable decline in student outcomes because of specific school policies that mitigated declining outcomes, rather than due to a substantively different experience for students. One could debate whether or not these, in fact, constitute strategies to mitigate the effects of violence on student outcomes. However, this is one of the reasons why we identified the effects of violence across multiple outcomes in selecting schools for in-depth interviews around school practices.

Teachers and students reported more supportive school climates in schools that mitigated declines in student outcomes

If schools can mitigate declines in academic outcomes for students living in proximity to homicide, we might expect that protectiveness to be related to aspects of educator practice and school climate and organization—such as strong instruction, attentiveness to relational trust, adult collaboration, and connectedness in the classroom.

To explore this possible relationship, we tested for statistical associations between school protectiveness and a selected subset of measures of school climate and organization that are available on the *5Essentials* student and teacher surveys.[75] We limited our analysis to 25 survey measures connected to previous research findings on protective factors in the lives of vulnerable young people and omitted measures that previous studies suggested were unlikely to be either consequentially or statistically related to school protectiveness. The research studies included on p.5-6 and Appendix A have additional contextual details.

Overall, our analyses found that:

- Schools that mitigated declines in student outcomes had broadly more positive measures of school climate than other schools;
- Schools that mitigated declines in GPAs, attendance, and behavioral outcomes were characterized by stronger survey reports across most survey measures. These included measures about engaging instruction and trusting, connected relationships with peers and teachers;
- Teachers' reports of school commitment and trust among teachers and with their principal were associated with preventing declines in GPAs and behavioral outcomes;
- Schools where teachers and students reported feeling safer, with fewer classroom disruptions, and less disorder and crime were less likely to have declines on most outcomes; and
- Only a few of the 25 survey measures analyzed were related to preventing declines on test scores.

The specific pattern of measures of school climate and organization that were related to protectiveness against declines varied slightly across student outcomes. A checked box in **Table 3** indicates that there was a statistically significant association between protective-

75 See p.5-6 in Chapter 1 and Appendix A for details on which measures were selected for analysis and why.

ness on the outcome (columns) and the indicated survey measures (rows). **Appendix A** describes each of the survey measures in detail. **Appendix D** provides the statistical correlations represented in **Table 3.**

The survey responses suggest that schools that mitigated the negative academic impacts of living in proximity to homicide were broadly characterized as having strong, engaging instruction and a climate of connected, trusting relationships among students, teachers, and school leadership. But what were the specific practices occurring in schools that supported stronger student and teacher reports? Chapter 6 examines reports from educators in three schools that were relatively more successful at mitigating the negative effects of living in close proximity to homicide, to show their strategies for supporting students exposed to traumatic events.

TABLE 3

Schools that mitigated the negative academic impacts of living in proximity to homicide had stronger measures of school climate and organization

	5Essentials Survey measures	Academic outcomes		Behavioral outcomes		
		GPA	Test scores	Infractions	Suspensions	Attendance
Student survey measures	Peer Support for Academic Work	☐	☑	☐	☐	☑
	Course Clarity	☑	☐	☑	☑	☑
	Emotional Health	☑	☐	☑	☑	☑
	Academic Engagement	☑	☐	☐	☐	☐
	Classroom Behavior	☑	☐	☑	☑	☑
	Classroom Personalism	☑	☐	☑	☐	☐
	Academic Press	☐	☐	☑	☑	☑
	School Connectedness	☑	☐	☑	☑	☑
	Classroom Rigor	☑	☐	☑	☑	☑
	Safety	☑	☐	☑	☑	☑
	School-level Academic Press	☑	☐	☑	☑	☑
	School Safety	☑	☐	☑	☑	☑
	Rigorous Study Habits	☐	☐	☑	☑	☐
	Student-Teacher Trust	☑	☐	☑	☑	☑
Teacher survey measures	Classroom Disruptions	☑	☑	☑	☑	☑
	Teacher Collaboration	☐	☐	☐	☐	☐
	Collective Responsibility	☑	☐	☑	☑	☐
	Teacher Influence	☑	☐	☐	☐	☐
	Instructional Leadership	☑	☐	☐	☐	☐
	Program Coherence	☑	☐	☑	☑	☑
	Reflective Dialogue	☑	☑	☐	☐	☐
	School Commitment	☑	☐	☑	☑	☑
	Teacher-Principal Trust	☑	☐	☑	☑	☐
	Teacher-Teacher Trust	☑	☐	☑	☑	☐
	Disorder and Crime	☑	☐	☑	☑	☑

Note: Check boxes indicate a statistically significant association between the high school's score on the measure and the school-specific size of the change in the noted outcome measure in years when students live in proximity to homicide compared with years when they do not. Appendix D provides the estimated associations. Test score data is limited for high schools because fewer standardized tests are given; the relatively few associations between protectiveness and survey measures is likely due to this data limitation. Analysis was based on school by year observations from 2010-11 through 2018-19 for the 557 schools meeting the sample criterion discussed in Chapter 1. Analysis is based on more than 1.35 million student-school year survey responses and about 178,000 teacher-school year survey responses. The average survey response rates were 79% for the student survey and 75% for the teacher survey. Appendix Table A.1. provides year and survey specific response rates.

CHAPTER 5

The Experiences and Perspectives of Adults in Schools that Mitigated Declines in Student Outcomes

We interviewed administrators, educators, and staff in three CPS high schools that mitigated the negative effects of proximity to homicide, identified through the quantitative analyses described on p.12 in Chapter 1. Our interviews focused on how adults organized and understood their work, with particular attention to how they approached the task of supporting students.

Chapter 5 highlighted key features of the climate and organization in schools that mitigated the negative effects of proximity to homicide. In this chapter, we explore three themes that emerged from interviews with educators, administrators, and school staff in three of these high schools:

1. Administrators, classroom teachers, and school staff described the work of behavioral health teams (BHTs) as an **integrated set of systems, structures, and routines that closely coordinated the work of adults** around addressing students' emotional wellness and mental health within a multi-tiered systems of support (MTSS) framework;
2. Administrators, educators, and school staff collectively described a school-wide focus on **intentionally fostering and sustaining strong, trusting relationships between students and adults**, emphasizing the value of restorative and inclusive practices to build and maintain a sense of social connectedness; and
3. Administrators and classroom educators together described the importance of, and effort devoted to, creating and sustaining a practice of **centering and directly addressing students' lived experiences** through the development of culturally responsive curriculum and instructional practice.

The findings in this chapter are drawn from qualitative data collected across the three CPS high schools. Of note, the measures of school organizational and climate analyzed in Chapter 4, **Table 3** were not used to select these three high schools. However, researchers analyzed survey results from these three schools after selection to confirm that the selected schools shared the characteristics of schools that play a protective role, as described in Chapter 4.[76]

This chapter provides a more detailed picture of what the practices and culture looked like in these three schools that had strong organizational climates and mitigated the negative effects of living in close proximity to homicide on students' academic performance.

76 All high schools selected for qualitative study were stronger than average on measures of teacher-student trust, teacher collaboration, and reflective dialog and weaker than average on the measure of school safety. Two of the three schools were also stronger than average on measures of classroom disruption (reflecting lower levels of disruption), collective responsibility instructional leadership, program coherence, and teacher trust. For a full discussion of qualitative site selection and description of the interview sample, please also see Chapter 1.

What this data does—and doesn't—offer

The experiences and perspectives of adults in these three schools are not representative across the school district; nor do they allow us to draw strong definite conclusions about what differentiates effective and ineffective schools. This analysis does not imply what educators should or should not do; rather, it underscores the notion that there are multiple pathways educators and schools may take to creating environments that mitigate the effects of living in close proximity to homicide on students' academic performance. Additionally, for practical and ethical reasons, the research team did not conduct interviews directly with students regarding their experiences with either homicide (or violence more broadly), nor regarding the specific supports they did or did not receive in school. Families and caregivers were also not interviewed for this project, although a number of educators whom we interviewed drew attention to the importance of partnering closely with families and caregivers as well. For this reason, the analysis presented is limited to the experiences and perspectives of adults in schools. Adults' reflections and this analysis expand our understanding of the choices adults make in their efforts to support students and the roles they may ultimately play in making schools responsive, healing-centered spaces for students. These findings are consistent with the quantitative analyses presented in the Chapter 4, which showed that across high schools, there were small declines in student outcomes in schools with strong school relationships and collaborative work.

1. Systematically addressing emotional wellness and mental health through Multi-tiered Systems of Support (MTSS)

Educators in the three high schools described using MTSS to organize their responses to students' emotional wellbeing and mental health needs. First described in a 1996 article in the *Journal of Emotional and Behavioral Health Disorders*, MTSS is a research-based, tiered framework, intended to provide educators and school staff with guidelines for providing appropriate, tailored instruction and interventions to support all students' success in school.[77] Since its inception, MTSS has gained widespread acceptance and the framework was included in the 2015 federal Every Student Succeeds Act as a school-wide approach to increasing teacher effectiveness and increasing student achievement that integrates differentiated instruction and social-emotional learning supports in a tiered or targeted framework.[78] In CPS, the district describes MTSS as "a framework that guides schools and teachers to provide appropriate instruction and interventions to ensure all students receive the education and supports they need to be successful in school."[79] "Tier 1" supports include core instruction and behavioral supports present for all students, while "tier 2" and "tier 3" supports are progressively more intensive and targeted instruction and behavioral supports provided to small groups or individuals, respectively. In CPS, all schools are expected to implement behavioral health teams within an MTSS framework, per district policy.

At the school level, effective implementation of MTSS relies on the effective operation of interprofessional teams, often referred to in schools as 'behavioral health teams' (BHTs). BHTs are described in the research literature as multi-disciplinary teams of adults that are conceived of as a strategy to maximize school mental health resources through collaboration among adults in using data to identify and match students with mental health needs to evidence-based interventions.[80] BHTs are tasked with assessing data on student performance and behavior (e.g., attendance, GPAs, credit accumulation, behavioral infractions, referrals, etc.), engaging in root cause analyses, and collaboratively developing strategies and interventions to meet students' needs. The assumed strength of BHTs working within tiered support frameworks, such as MTSS, is that they enable adults to identify, address, and evaluate the needs of individuals and groups of students in timely, targeted, and effective ways in order to ensure that all students receive effective, appropriate mental health services.

77 Walker & Horner (1996).
78 Thurlow, Ghere, Lazarus, & Liu (2020); Walker & Horner (1996).
79 Chicago Public Schools (n.d.a.).
80 Raviv et al. (2022).

31

Importantly, previous research on the implementation of expanded school mental health approaches, including MTSS and BHTs, notes a number of practical challenges to their effective use in schools. On the one hand, research evidence suggests that effective mental health services in schools can operate as a gateway through which students ultimately gain access to additional resources and supports.[81] On the other hand, studies suggest that educators and schools may face significant challenges in implementing MTSS and BHTs, including issues with workforce capacity and training, as well as competing priorities (e.g., instructional goals), and difficulty sharing information across systems.[82] Coordinating services across all three tiers is complex and difficult work and previous research suggests that educators and schools may struggle with inadequate guidance around selecting and implementing interventions at different tiers, making it difficult to match students to appropriate services.[83] Previous research suggests that educators and schools may also lack strong guidance on how to form and maintain effective multidisciplinary teams and that this may be particularly true in chronically under-resourced schools, which also frequently serve communities with limited access to mental health care more broadly.[84] In spite of these issues, however, there is growing evidence to support the adoption and use of these approaches as effective means of expanding students' access to mental health services in schools.[85]

BHTs reported relying on trust and coordination between adults to systematically identify, monitor, and provide targeted supports for students' emotional wellness and mental health within an MTSS framework. Within the three high schools, administrators, educators, and school staff described the deliberate use of BHTs to anchor and foster close, interconnected schoolwide networks of adults that focused intently on monitoring students' emotional wellness and mental health. As interprofessional teams often led by counselors, interviewees described BHTs as playing a critical role in not only monitoring student wellness, but also in organizing communication across educators in the schools and supporting their collaboration in addressing student needs. As one counselor explained, members of BHTs intentionally placed themselves at the center of carefully coordinated, consistent communication efforts, designed both to prevent students from falling through the cracks and to coordinate adults' responses:

> *"I'm glued to my phone... and I think that's what the teachers really appreciate. And that's why they say 'The counselors are awesome!' We keep them updated. They're not [out of] the loop with anything. And vice versa... I'll update teachers that say 'the student was gone.' And I'll send an email to all [that student's] teachers—'Hey, [this] student was absent—please allow them to make up any work.' That's the communication with [the teachers]."*

Members of BHTs described their work as not only emphasizing clear, consistent communication, but also as focused on building and sustaining strong, underlying relationships between adults to cement systematic responses to student needs. As one counselor on a BHT at a different school explained, she focused deliberately on creating rapport and building a foundation of trust with her colleagues early in the year in order to support their shared work with students:

> *"So, up front, literally the first week [of school], I made a point to [build trust] and just share [with teachers] why I'm here, who I am. [Let them know that] if they have any questions, [they can] email or find me. This is my room number. Whatever. And I think that over time, they have come to know that when something happens, I will be listening to them.... I'm always present if a crisis does come up... And they will contact me when things happen... [because]... I will follow up [immediately]. I'm not just like, 'Oh, okay. I'll take of that later.'"*

81 Farmer, Burns, Phillips, Angold, & Costello (2003); Raviv et al. (2022).
82 Mellin, Taylor, & Weist (2014); Raviv et al. (2022); Stephan, Weist, Kataoka, Adelsheim, & Mills (2007).
83 Anderson & Borgmeier (2010); Domitrovich et al. (2008); Eiraldi et al. (2019); Raviv et al. (2022).
84 Kittelman, McIntosh, & Hoselton (2019); Raviv et al. (2022); Taylor & Adelman (2000).
85 Farmer et al. (2003); Raviv et al. (2022).

Trust between adults was critically important to how they understood and experienced the work of BHTs. As interviewees described it, the combination of up-front, transparent communication between adults and being consistently present for students was core to the work of clearly articulating, coordinating, and reliably executing plans to support students identified as in need. In turn, communication, trust, and coordination across adults was seen as key to ensuring that the work of BHTs was understood to be shared work across all staff, rather than the siloed responsibilities of a handful of counselors or administrators. This set of approaches contributed to a general view of BHTs in these three schools as a transparent, well-understood, and reliable pathway to ensuring that students' needs were being met. As one classroom educator explained, *"I know that if I ever can't handle a situation... if this is something that's simply beyond my scope as a teacher... I know exactly who to reach out to."*

The high degree of transparency and trust in these systems was also viewed as critical to their effectiveness in monitoring and identifying students' needs, on the one hand, and matching them to appropriate resources and supports, on the other. Adults we interviewed felt that high levels of trust among members of the BHT was especially important to sustaining their ongoing engagement with the emotionally difficult work of supporting students, particularly in school contexts that often appeared on the surface to be defined by a constant collision of high, unmet student need and perennially constrained and insufficient resources. In order to keep adults invested in the face of the many challenges students were facing, BHTs had to create and sustain the common conviction that their work was not only shared, but strategic and impactful.

During the COVID-19 pandemic and the move to remote learning, interviewees reported that many of these dense, interconnected networks of adult relationships and coordinated responses became significantly more difficult to maintain. Though BHTs worked to transfer their formal coordination of MTSS into the remote context, some people felt that many of the core practices of communication, rapport building, and close collaboration among adults in schools were disrupted and strained. Where their efforts to support and sustain communication and coordination across adults were absent or less effective, even in schools that remained protective for students, educators came to view MTSS as less effective in meeting students' needs.

One classroom educator explained that, in the midst of the pandemic and the move to remote and hybrid work, without that close communication and coordination among adults, MTSS sometimes came to seem like *"an empty hole"* into which they threw referral after referral, with little sense of *"who will reply at the end of it."* Adults' sense of isolation from each other, as well as from their students, seemed to almost palpably unwind BHTs' careful work of creating and sustaining those dense, interconnected networks that appeared to be so critical to the impactful implementation of MTSS in our three field site schools.

Adults described closely coordinated provision of tier 2 and tier 3 services via ongoing partnerships with external, community-based organizations (CBOs) and service providers to extend the impact of limited resources. Administrators, educators, and school staff (e.g., counselors, social workers) described operating within contexts of seemingly extreme resource constraint. Schools in our qualitative sample typically had at least one, and often more than one, full-time counselor and social worker. These individuals were often described as critically important to the larger work of the school and were frequently placed at the center of descriptions of the work of BHTs. However, there was a broad awareness across adults we interviewed that although having dedicated, full-time behavioral health professionals on staff was critically important, students' emotional wellness and mental health needs significantly exceeded what even a well-staffed team, much less a single individual, could effectively address. As a result, close, coordinated work between BHTs and external organizations around tier 2 and tier 3 service provision were described as a vital means of extending the capacity of schools to address students' needs. As one counselor explained, part of the work of the BHT also included organizing and coordinating partnerships with external, CBO providers, many of whom provided tier 2 and tier 3 services directly to students, but otherwise lacked mechanisms for sharing information or coordinating efforts to serve particular students:

33

"We talk about [coordination] in the BHT. We have a monthly meeting where it's an open meeting [and] we invite all [of our community] partners just so that they [can] share any updates. We have BAM and WOW [that] comes in; we have YMCA... They [all] come in like, 'Hey, these are the trends that we're seeing' or visa versa. [Sometimes] they need help from us." [86]

These types of close, coordinated partnerships between BHTs and CBOs were described as present in all three schools in which we conducted fieldwork. Within the MTSS framework, these partnerships typically focused on extending schools' capacity by providing additional tier 2 and tier 3 services. In some instances, these CBO partnerships were characterized as allowing these schools to provide additional services and/or accommodations to students above and beyond what the school itself was otherwise able and/or legally required to provide. In other instances, CBO partnerships were described as allowing these schools to increase the number of students receiving tier 2 and tier 3 services, beyond what the school had resources to sustain. Although in some instances these partnerships were longer-running over a period of years, many of the connections between schools and CBOs were contingent on the availability of resources to support the CBOs' involvement. As a result, partnerships between CBOs and schools were vital, but periodically unstable parts of the infrastructure within these school communities.

The ability to deepen available services and expand services to larger numbers of students were viewed as valuable dimensions of CBO partnership in all three of these schools. However, administrators were particularly aware that deepening and extending targeted services at tiers 2 and 3 did not necessarily lead to the development of a coherent, integrated school-wide program that served all students at tier 1. As valuable as tier 2 and tier 3 services clearly were in our sample schools, one school administrator explained how limited their impact remained on most students, as well as on the long-run development of the school community as a whole:

"So many of those things that have been prescribed along the way—we have seen so many of them come and go. So many initiatives. So many agencies or organizations that have played key role in one moment and then disappeared the next... because very few really take the time to understand what it means when we say "a student's lived experience" or "affirming students" [racial] or cultural identity."

In addition to administrators' concerns about the limited impact of focusing heavily on their schools' tier 2 and 3 services, counselors expressed similar concerns about both the impact of that focus on their workload, and their effectiveness in meaningfully shifting students' experience across the school as a whole. In most instances, counselors and social workers in these schools described investing heavily in the communication and coordination of BHTs to support student services, and splitting time individually serving large caseloads, often of 100 students or more. In addition, counselors and social workers described bearing the primary responsibility for managing the substantial volume of paperwork and documentation associated with planning and delivering services to students. This complex burden of planning, delivering, coordinating, and monitoring/documenting the extension of more targeted and intensive tier 2 and tier 3 services often left counselors in these schools feeling like they had little time and energy, as well as insufficient resources, to support the development and implementation of school-wide (tier 1) efforts aimed at all students:

"It's really tough, trying to build relationships [with students and teachers]... we're trying to be in the classrooms more often, collaborate with teachers, show face in as many different settings [as we can], but it's definitely a challenge... We have a lot of paperwork. A big part of the job is documentation and data analysis and intervention planning—things that happen behind the scenes that then take away [from] the time that we have to be proactively reaching out to students. I wish that [reaching out to students] were the only part

86 Becoming a Man (BAM) and Working on Womanhood (WOW) are school-based youth counseling programs run by Youth Guidance.

of the job, but unfortunately, I also lead our behavioral health team and there's a lot that comes with that, coordinating partnerships... it's time-consuming and gets in the way of what we're able to do directly with kids."

Adults felt confident in providing coordinated, targeted tier 2 and tier 3 services, but struggled more to define, develop, and implement coherent, school-wide tier 1 programs. Administrators, educators, and school staff were confident and clear in articulating their approach to and practices of BHTs to support coordination and service delivery to students identified as needing tier 2 and tier 3 services. This familiarity and confidence contrasted sharply with their individual and collective frustration with the limitations of their efforts to develop and implement effective school-wide (tier 1) efforts aimed at all students. Many of the services provided at tier 2 and tier 3, whether by school staff or through coordinated CBO partnerships, were discrete, manualized, a la carte interventions. In contrast, administrators and BHT members characterized tier 1 efforts as ambiguous, longer-term, and multi-pronged investments with frequently unclear or seemingly uncertain outcomes. In many instances, interviewees loosely described vaguely complementary approaches to mixing and matching restorative justice approaches, social emotional learning curricula, and trauma-informed practices together under the tier 1 umbrella, but without a clear, concrete articulation of the fit between the various pieces.

One administrator paused to call out their analysis of their own internal data, which showed how ineffective efforts to tie things like students' attendance and GPAs to incentives like school dances and other special privileges had been. Those sorts of incentive-focused strategies to create school-wide supports for students, he explained, *"are a lot of work... cost us a lot of money, and we don't get a lot of bang for our buck."* Pointing to their work at tier 2 and tier 3 as a strength, he continued: *"those students typically self-identify based on their behavior,"* enabling adults to wrap around them and ramp up targeted supports as needed. Tier 1 school-wide efforts, on the other hand, represented a major weakness, which he characterized as *"very lacking,"* largely because it consisted of little more than small, disconnected initiatives, *"but nothing that's really meaty."*

The perception that students "self-identify" for tier 2 and tier 3 supports based on behavior was a consistent theme across interviews in all three of the high schools in which we collected data. This belief appeared to reflect the logic of BHTs' practice of closely monitoring data on student performance and particularly student behavior—often classroom educators' assessments of that behavior, rather than any direct observation of it—as a proxy for mental health needs and a pretext for referral to tier 2 and tier 3 services. When adults described their practices, tier 2 and 3 services appeared to be a response to student behavior. In contrast, adults' thinking about tier 1 reflected a focus on preventative measures, aimed at reducing the need for tier 2 and tier 3 services. Further, that a tier 1 school-wide approach to responding to students emotional and mental wellbeing should be grounded in efforts to substantively improve relationships across the school community. As one administrator observed, even the most effective triage and case management system imaginable would be unlikely to fundamentally shift the entire school community:

"We have referrals [for tier 2 and 3]; there's a referral process. And if something [is] outside the scope of someone's work here [at the school], we connect students and families with external resources and partners. And we do work with BAM and WOW and other agencies within the school to provide maybe more intensive interventions. But ultimately, it's not okay, or feasible, to think that a counseling team... and social workers... even though that's a lot more than most schools have... are going to really do anything super effective [for school-wide impact]. You're not going to bring anything to scale."

These remarks reflected the prevailing sense of adults in the schools where we conducted interviews; that tier 2 and tier 3 services were simultaneously essential and insufficient. Adults reflected on the importance of having what they often described as a "targeted impact" on those smaller groups and individual students who required the most resource- and time-intensive forms of support. But many adults we interviewed also pointed to important, albeit less formally coordinated efforts taking place among educators and students within classrooms. Adults across these three schools emphasized the importance of school-wide efforts to attend directly to students in their classrooms in real time. As the next two sections demonstrate, the work occurring within classrooms to sustain relationships with students and center students' lived experiences was characterized as essential to connecting efforts at tier 2 and tier 3 to the broader work of addressing students school-wide at tier 1.

2. Intentionally fostering and sustaining inclusive, trusting relationships

The experiences and perspectives of adults in the three high schools where we conducted interviews suggest that the quality of relationships and support students experienced in their schools reflected considerable time, energy, and creativity on the part of adults in those schools. The educators we interviewed repeatedly emphasized the value they placed on fostering and sustaining strong, trusting relationships with students. This emphasis on trust and connection extended into specific efforts to adopt empathetic and holistic orientations to students' social-emotional needs and to prioritize inclusive responses to students' behavior in classrooms and schools.

Educators and school staff reported intentionally fostering and deepening trusting relationships by adopting an empathetic and holistic orientation toward the social-emotional needs of all students. While mental health providers on BHTs often centered the importance of relationships and trust in clinical settings, educators and administrators also described a broader emphasis on adopting empathetic and holistic orientations toward students' social-emotional needs in order to promote a stronger sense of interconnection and belonging.

As one administrator explained, a multi-tiered service framework like MTSS can help provide guidance around how to support individual students with specific needs, but *"at some point,"* the work of adults in schools is more fundamentally about *"developmental relationships... about understanding your role and your place in the world of a particular student."* The emphasis on relationships and trust between adults and students, he explained, formed the core of their school-wide approach to responding to student needs and in fact, underpinned more targeted efforts in classrooms and clinical settings:

> *"We focus heavily on relationships and whenever things start to break down, the first thing I ask is 'So what is your relationship with this child? What do we know about them outside of school? What is their home life like?' These are the questions we ask, because if you don't know the child, then I don't know how you expect us to really get far in our interventions. So, our interventions are going to be based on relationships. That's it."*

Adults in the three high schools in which we conducted interviews described efforts to leverage adults who were strong social connectors or enjoyed particularly close, trusting relationships with students. As one educator observed, adults in her school were frequently in the habit of asking each other *"Hey, who knows this kid?"* in order to figure out who among them they could rely on to reach students in need of support. Adults in the school, she continued, also believed it was their collective responsibility to *"creating space"* for students' emotional lives within classrooms and the school. Interviewees characterized this intentional relational work as a complement to the frequently more focused, data-driven monitoring of students that BHTs regularly engaged in. One teacher described her work in the classroom as *"empathetic listening,"* explaining that her focus was less on *"asking probing questions"* but more just on *"creating a space [for students] to express themselves, [to] let me know what's going on, and how it feels."* Short of beginning more formal processes of referring students in distress to existing structures like the BHT—which might escalate a situation while also pulling in additional resources and supports—a number of adults described just listening directly and without judgment to students. One administrator described his practice as:

> *"Just being an ear for [students]. A lot of these things [that they're experiencing], they cannot control. The thing that I think I have deal with most*

[with students] is processing. Processing those things—kids try to blame themselves for things happening. And it's like, 'No, this has nothing to do with you.' They have some guilt... I make sure that I ask them the proper questions, give them the time to vent, give advice, just make sure they feel comfortable in the space [so that they can do the things they need to do]."

Educators and school staff reported emphasizing restorative responses to students that fostered and maintained a sense of connectedness and relational trust. Building on their descriptions of intentional investments in creating strong, trusting relationships with students, educators across the three high schools in which we conducted interviews also underscored their view of the importance of creating policies and practices in classrooms that emphasized creating and maintaining connection and relationship between adults and young people. In particular, the educators we interviewed highlighted the importance of maintaining and/or restoring connection with students throughout and particularly after conflicts, disagreements, or disruptions emerged in the classroom. One educator described how his classroom practice had evolved to more deliberately slow down, to focus on, and to center students' experiences in addressing disruption. As he explained:

"I'm able to zoom in and zoom out. I'm able to listen and then zoom out and try to see, "What is actually being said here? How can I distill the actual issue that's going on here?" In that instance, the impulse is just to keep moving on, but if you can find a space to figure out what's going on... it's really helpful."

Educators in the three high schools repeatedly reported using restorative practices, such as talking circles, peer mediation, and reparative consequences to create inclusive, supportive classroom communities that downplayed reliance on exclusionary disciplinary practices, such an in- or out-of-school suspensions. Restorative justice approaches are broadly described in the literature in terms of a clear emphasis on collectively repairing harm, rather than punishing individuals for actions that disrupt or damage the community in some form or fashion.[87] Evidence on the effectiveness of restorative justice approaches in schools suggests that such practices may have positive impacts on school climate and produce reductions in misconduct and the use of exclusionary discipline (e.g., suspensions, expulsions).[88]

Among interviewees, the use of restorative responses was described as another opportunity for educators to intentionally orchestrate classroom community and, as one interviewee put it, a chance *"to develop a second family for student[s]. "You have 30 other people in a room that can be a family to this kid,"* that can support them, he explained. As interviewees observed, students who were struggling needed more resources and supports, not fewer. The emphasis on restorative responses to students was also repeatedly and explicitly cited as important to reducing educators' reliance on excluding students from classrooms or from school. As another educator explained:

"I really try to develop a classroom environment where work can take place. I'm not a fan of handing students off no matter how bad it gets. I really try to make it a point to never send a kid down to the dean's office. The one time that I did, I went with the student. I sat down there in the office with her to talk it out and stuff. Obviously, I want to recognize my limitations and where I've reached a point where it's like, 'okay this is a big, big deal. I probably need to work with somebody else right now. I need somebody else to help me support this student.' But I really do try..."

In addition to promoting a strong sense of inclusive classroom community and reducing educators' reliance on exclusionary disciplinary practices, interviewees also believed that restorative responses to students reduced the burden placed on other structures within

87 Pavelka (2013).
88 Darling-Hammond, Fronius, Sutherland, Guckenburg, Petrosino, & Hurley (2020).

the school, including counselors and the BHTs. By emphasizing connectedness and inclusivity at the classroom level through restorative responses to students, educators in the three schools described that they freed up the time and energy of other adults in the school to focus more resources and support on the smaller number of students with more acute needs.

Beyond the classroom, counselors and community partners in the three high schools often explicitly highlighted similar efforts to build strong, mutualistic, and trusting relationships with students. A community partner who facilitated small group counseling sessions in one of the schools explained that his effort to be responsive to students often resonated quickly with them. *"They understand that it's a love and respect relationship,"* he offered. As a result, he explained, students become *"open to discuss with me anything that's pertaining to their personal life."* The emphasis on openness and trust in the efforts of community partners paralleled efforts of educators in classrooms to reduce reliance on punitive, exclusionary disciplinary practices. The same individual reflected that, while students may not always appreciate the effort in the moment, the deliberate emphasis on restorative responses to students over time reinforced a sense of mutualism and trust between adults and young people. He explained:

> *"As much as they complain and might not like when we redirect them or we have restorative justice practices, they may not like it sometimes, but however, they appreciate it because it's what gives us the respect... So being honest with them is actually what makes the job more warm and welcoming because they become open to you at all places and times."*

Taken together, educators across the three schools viewed restorative responses to students in classrooms as a way to foster and maintain students' connection to their classrooms, their peers, and to their teachers. Educators and staff across the three schools underscored the value of explicit efforts to downplay excluding students from classrooms and schools when and where disruptions did occur, noting that it both reinforced a sense of mutual respect between adults and young people and kept students in the classrooms where they belonged. The extensive discussion of restorative responses to students was noteworthy for all it contained, but also for what it lacked. Across all 29 interviews, including conversations with administrators, classroom educators, counselors, and community partners alike, interviewees rarely characterized students as "disruptive" or "misbehaved," nor used phrases such as "misconduct" or "discipline."

Centering and addressing students' lived experiences through curriculum and instruction.

In our interviews, classroom educators in particular described deliberate efforts to center students' lived experiences through curriculum and instruction, as means to create relevant, engaging experiences within the classroom. These classroom experiences, in turn, were also explicitly intended to foster the development of students' own critical awareness of the world and events surrounding them.

Adults reported centering and addressing students' lived experiences in classrooms in order to foster students' engagement and encourage critical analyses of their experiences outside of school. As one educator explained, particularly against the backdrop of the COVID-19 pandemic and the emergence of nationwide protests taking place at the same time against policy violence directed at people of color, these choices were not in lieu of addressing traditional course content, but rather represented efforts to deliberately position the school and its classrooms at the center of students' efforts to make sense of the forces shaping their lives:

> *"[We're] educating kids, not just on like algebra, but like educating them on things that matter to them and impact their day- to -day lives. I'm thinking, like our civics class, which is a junior level class: they did like a whole unit on social movements and forms of protest and civil disobedience... that's what the kids were learning about and engaging with... [We're] thinking about schools as the place where, you know, students become connected to people, to resources, to ideas... it's a beautiful picture."*

As another teacher explained, students' lives are *"impacted by a lot of racial issues, by a lot of policing issues, a lot of gun violence."* For many students, schools and classrooms are critically important spaces for *"validating their experiences and giving them space to express themselves."* The use of curriculum and instruction to create supportive spaces for meaning making, she concluded, *"gives [students] a way to deal with,"* to make sense of, and to respond constructively to what are often emotionally difficult and deeply unsettling experiences.

The practice of centering students' lived experiences in curriculum and instruction, however important, remained something that many teachers described as difficult, demanding, and ongoing work for them, personally and professionally. For many teachers, particularly those teaching across differences of race and class, the challenge of centering their students' lived experiences forced them into complex, sometimes difficult reflections on how their own identities and their own lived experiences as young people in schools shaped their expectations and behavior in the classroom. As one teacher explained, *"trying to be sensitive to what's happening in the kids' lives... in [developing] lessons,"* working to center students' lived experiences outside of school in their work within in, required teachers to confront many of their own assumptions about their students, about what their lives were actually like. In turn, she explained, that confrontation pushed teachers to reflect on how they approached and interacted with students, altering not only what teachers taught and how, but also an entire manner of relating to students (discussed in greater detail on p. 37 in the section describing restorative practices).

Teachers described the work of centering students' lived experiences and supporting their analyses and sense-making as a discipline that required careful, sustained personal and professional reflection. As one teacher asserted, that reflective work is *"super important"* and constant. She described her own sustained practice of reflection—keeping notes and journaling; producing what she described as *"written testimony"* for herself of her own experiences working to develop opportunities and supports for students' sense making—as critically important to *"create[ing] sustainable change and awareness."* The reflective work, the work of building classrooms that respond to and support students' efforts to make sense of their lives beyond school, she explained bluntly, *"starts with me."*

Adults described intentionally soliciting, engaging, and incorporating students' voices and leadership into the design and execution of classroom activities. Interviewees described how centering students lived experience in curriculum development and classroom instruction required them to engage students as partners in design. The educators we interviewed described actively working to encourage and support students in choosing topics and activities directly connected to the current and historical realities of their lives, their families, and their communities. As with efforts to center students' lived experiences in curriculum and instruction, educators and school staff frequently described the work of incorporating student voice and leadership in their classrooms as a disruptive, challenging, but ultimately vital force in making (and remaking) their classrooms to be more responsive to their students' intellectual and emotional sense-making needs. One educator explained the interconnected nature of the challenge facing adults in making classrooms and schools more responsive to students:

> *"If we want everything to be centered around young people, adults have to learn to step back. I think that that's a big lesson that it's hard for adults to do, and I think that when you start to do that, there's a whole other brilliance that happens and it's addicting. It's like you can never go back. But until you make that decision, it's so hard for adults to release control in that way."*

Educators and school staff described moves toward including students in meaningful, consequential decision-making around a range of issues. In one of the three schools, an administrator noted that efforts to include students as design partners in the work of the school had extended beyond not only choices about curriculum and instruction, but also to ongoing discussions regarding grading and other aspects of school policy. Beginning from more modest efforts to engage students in designing classroom projects around their own lived experiences and interests, he explained, students were now regularly included as members of a number of committees, reviewing, discussing, and sometimes modifying school policy alongside and in partnership with their teachers and administrators.

These efforts were challenging for educators and administrators alike, often running counter to long-established ways of organizing and wielding authority in classrooms and schools. One educator reflected that although *"there [was] generally an effort to include students"* in decision-making, the school itself was still struggling to create what they described as a culture of inclusion. *"There have been a lot of times this year,"* the same teacher reflected, *"where decisions are being made and someone will bring up... 'What do students think about this? Shouldn't we ask the people that we're planning this for?"* Educators across these three high schools reflected on the power and promise of this approach.

During the pandemic, efforts were made to center not only the lived experiences but also the voice and leadership of students as well. The educators and school staff in our sample described the active role that student leaders in their schools took in organizing efforts to support families across the school and the wider communities served. In one school, student leaders organized a food pantry that provided groceries to families experiencing sporadic unemployment and food insecurity as a result of the pandemic. The food pantry was underwritten by a mutual aid society, itself set up and funded by students and teachers together at the school.

Educators reported adopting pedagogical approaches designed to center and honor students' cultural identities. In addition to centering the lived experiences of students and actively incorporating student voice and leadership into the design of curriculum, instruction, and school policy, the educators and school staff in our sample also extended those practices by adopting culturally-responsive and culturally-sustaining pedagogies that centered and honored students' cultural identities and cultural wealth. Educators and administrators of color in those three schools reflected on the strong sense of affinity that guided their affirmations of students' cultural identities and cultural wealth. One Latina educator reflected on the way in which affirming her students' cultural identity and cultural wealth in and through her teaching represented a commitment to fully realizing students' agency and potential in her classroom, but also far beyond it:

> *"That is what I have experienced, what I have seen other people, my people, experience is that when we are affirmed in who we are in our identity and when we are strong in what we know, and who we are, and where we come from, the sky's the limit ... [Students] should determine what that is. That's my thing. Not other people determining what that is. That is our autonomy, that is our sovereignty, and that's our self-determination."*

Educators believed that affirming students' cultural identities was connected to recognizing and realizing their agency, their potential, and their humanity. They also described how this approach to curriculum and instruction could be transformative, extending beyond creating classrooms and school spaces that were merely responsive to the experiences and needs of students. As a Latino administrator reflected:

> *"It is mind blowing to be able to then organize, or reorganize the school to really reflect a student's lived experience. Because in that lived experience, there is so much hope and so much power, so much resilience, a lot of pain, but a lot of love. And all of that is in that student's humanity. And if I can create a school where that humanity is not only validated, it's recognized, but lifted up, then that student, even [if] he had just experienced something violent, will rise above that. Will rise above that. And knowing that [our school community] had a role to play in that is really what moves me."*

While educators and administrators of color reflected on the strong sense of racial and cultural affinity that guided their approaches, the White teachers we interviewed more often reflected on their status as privileged outsiders in many of the school communities in which they served. As one White male educator explained:

> *"At the end of the day, we are here to serve students. I don't live in this community, and I know a lot of our teachers don't... I look at it as I'm an honored guest in this community, and it is my job to serve the community and not think that I am any type of savior, or here to fix anyone, or... I know that there are so many assets and just a wealth of*

historic knowledge, cultural knowledge, wisdom, innovation, especially here in [this community]... I am here really in service of the school and the school community. And I have seen how brilliant and innovative and creative our young people are, and that inspires me, and our adults too."

"My job [as a teacher]," he continued, *"is really trying to surface and tap into [students'] talents and then help make connections and create opportunities for those to be showcased,"* for students, their families, and their communities to be affirmed, and for those talents to translate into contributions beyond the classroom and the school.

The understanding of teaching as facilitative, rather than merely didactic, represented a core element of the culturally-responsive and sustaining pedagogical approach described in interviews across these three high schools. This facilitative, culturally-engaged stance was reflected multiple times over in educators' rejection of deficit-based, damage-centering narratives about students, their families, and their communities. As one Latinx educator explained, repudiating the view of students as *"empty vessels, or at best, broken vessels that need to be fixed"* was at the core of recognizing and capitalizing on the wealth *"of creativity, of history, of knowledge, and experiences and skills"* that students, families, and communities bring to schools every day. The work of teaching, she continued, *"[is] not about filling anything up,"* but rather, consists daily of *"learning where [students] are at"* in their development and then *"building them up in the process."*

Interpretive Summary

This report offers evidence that schools can, and do, mitigate the negative impacts of adversity that young people experience. At the same time, this is complex, resource-intensive, and emotionally-taxing work—requiring time, resources and intentional strategies.

Elected, civic, and community leaders in Chicago and across the country can consider:

To create greater educational equity in Chicago, there is a clear need for greater public investment in addressing the epidemic of gun violence and the broader, longstanding historical disinvestment in communities of color throughout the city. Violence in Chicago, as elsewhere, is closely associated with long-standing and intentionally racialized policies of social and economic isolation and neglect that have systematically concentrated poverty and hardship in communities of color over generations. Chicago remains one of the most racially segregated cities in the U.S. The concentration of high levels of crime, gun violence, and homicide in many of those same communities is not incidental. These patterns of violence and poverty directly influence student achievement on multiple dimensions, and we found long-term effects on test scores of living in close proximity to violence that accumulate over time.

The findings from this report suggest that educators and schools can play important roles in the lives of young people who live in communities experiencing high levels of violence.

But while schools can play a vital role, it is critical to recognize that the will and the resources to address the scope and scale of the violence occurring in Chicago must necessarily be significantly wider than the school system alone. These efforts must be significant to turn the tide against an epidemic of gun violence that remains centered in some of the most economically and socially isolated communities in the city. Responsibility for addressing—and more importantly, preventing—violence and its disparate impacts, particularly in communities of color, must become a far more broadly shared mission across the city as a whole.

Insulating students from harm and promoting their resilience requires intentional, coordinated, and sustained effort. Schools can play a role in the lives of students who experience adversity in their lives outside of school. Schools that mitigated the negative effects of proximity to homicide were marked by well-coordinated systems of support, including behavioral health teams, and by strong, creative, and comprehensive approaches to building and sustaining relational trust. The intentional, coordinated, and sustained efforts of educators matter and, as this report shows, can mitigate some of the well-established negative effects of living in close proximity to homicide on students' academic trajectories. However, as this report highlights, the experiences and perspectives of educators working in schools that appeared to mitigate the negative effects of proximity to homicide suggest that this work is difficult and emotionally exhausting. Even in schools that mitigated the impact of adversity, educators frequently felt that their work was insufficient and that they were somehow not doing enough. The complexity of the work and the level of sustained coordination required to provide this level of support and care for students is terrific and takes an enormous toll on the adults who take responsibility for providing it.

Building strong, effective school culture and climate remains one of the most important and most basic elements of creating more responsive, resilient school communities. While specific evidence-based interventions and programs exist to extend the efforts of school leaders, educators, and staff, the findings from this report also highlight the importance of sustained investment in building the fundamental quality of schools' culture and climate. Strong school culture and climate across multiple measures was consistently associated with schools' ability to mitigate the negative effects of living in close geographical proximity to homicide on students' academic performance.

Providing resources and supports for the mental health and wellness of adults is a vital investment in the success of efforts to create responsive, student-centered school communities. The mental health, wellness, and resilience of adults (e.g., administrators, educators, school staff, community partners, and families and caregivers, etc.) is also a vitally important resource for creating and sustaining protective, thriving school communities. In schools that were more successful at mitigating the negative effects of proximity to homicide, we saw evidence of adults' efforts to build trust with students, but also to support and build trust with one another in the face of difficult work. Previous studies show how educators are also affected by their students' ACES outside of school. Terms like vicarious or "secondary" trauma have been used to describe the ways in which the mental health, wellness, and job performance of educators can be negatively affected by the impact of unaddressed adversity and stress in the lives of students.[89] A number of the school leaders and educators we interviewed for this project reflected on the emotional toll that their work with students took on them. Against the backdrop of media coverage of educator burnout and growing teacher turnover across the country, these reflections suggest that there is considerable work to be done ensuring that the approaches developed to ensure students' mental health and wellness also include resources and supports for the adults who care for them, as well. The needs of families and caregivers must also be addressed more broadly, keeping in mind that they are experiencing the stresses of living in close proximity to homicide themselves, while also managing myriad other challenges at the same time. Families and caregivers remain a primary resource for students and they require investment and support.

Strong, effective school leadership plays an important role creating school communities that respond consistently to the needs of students experiencing adversity. As shown in Chapter 4, the degree to which educators in a school believed their principal communicated a clear vision, understood what was happening in their classrooms, held clear, high expectations for their practice, and supported them professionally all were associated with whether a school mitigated the negative effects of adversity. The extent to which educators believed their principals afforded them a meaningful say in school policy, including over how the school approached curricular and instructional decisions as well as how it responded to student behavior, was also directly related to the capacity of schools to mitigate the negative impact of adversity on students' performance. Educators' belief that their principals provided coordination, consistency, and continuity in setting, implementing, and coordinating programs and approaches within the school was also characteristic of schools that insulated students from the negative effects of proximity to homicide. Strong trust between educators and principals appeared to be a critical resource that distinctively marked the climate and organization of these schools. The role of the principal in setting a vision and coordinating work across programs and teams is particularly important given the need for effective approaches to implementing multi-tiered systems of support (MTSS) and behavioral health teams (BHTs). Prior research has shown that program coordination is an essential role for the principal, distinguishing those who are effective at improving students' academic outcomes from those who are not.[90]

89 Christian-Brandt, Santacrose, & Barnett (2020); Essary, Barza, & Thurston (2020).

90 Gordon & Hart (2022).

Efforts to identify and respond to students' needs in a timely, effective manner appear to hinge on the capacity of adults to act in coordinated, coherent, and reliable ways. Previous research on the use of MTSS frameworks and structures such as BHTs highlight the importance of creating and sustaining systematic approaches to centering and responding to students' experiences and needs in schools. School leadership provides a crucially important anchor for developing and sustaining coordinated, coherent systems and structures within schools. The findings from this report provide further evidence that reliable systems that enable adults to monitor students' academic performance and behavior are a critical tool for creating responsive, student-centered school communities that effectively insulate students from the negative impact of adversity on their performance in school. These efforts rely not only on the close, coordinated efforts of educators and school staff, but also on creating and maintaining close working relationships between these schools and an array of community-based organizations (CBOs) and service providers with whom they partner. Maintaining (and expanding) deliberate and ongoing coordination, particularly between adults in schools and partners in the wider community, is complex and difficult work that requires time, energy, and resources to support. Educators do not and cannot do this work alone.

The relatively small number of schools most acutely affected by violence likely require greater resources and support to address students' needs. Violence affects students and schools across the city; however, a small subset of schools served substantial concentrations of students who lived in close geographic proximity to homicide, often multiple times in a single school year. The magnitude of the challenges facing this subset of schools points to the importance of providing additional resources in targeted ways that address the specific needs of those students and school communities in which the issues of violence and its impacts are more concentrated and pressing.

Partnerships with CBOs and service providers appeared to extend schools' capacity to identify and respond to students' needs. In schools that mitigated the negative effects of proximity violence, administrators and educators described their reliance on, and gratitude for, these close partnerships and underscored the importance of maintaining those ties in providing services to students. At the same time, CBOs and service providers also faced considerable funding and resource constraints. Bolstering partnerships between schools and CBOs and service providers with additional resources and supports, on the one hand, and removing obstacles to providing care on the other, appears to be an important avenue for continuing to strengthen and extend the impact of schools in the lives of vulnerable young people.

Efforts to more effectively resource and support partnerships may also be an important opportunity to improve connections more broadly between schools and the students, families, and communities whom they serve and, as such, represent an undercapitalized resource in increasing the effectiveness of schools on multiple fronts. Educators and administrators talked at length in our qualitative interviews about the importance of partnering effectively not only with CBOs, but also with families and caregivers more broadly. The role of families and caregivers in supporting students and particularly in these partnerships is also deserving of greater exploration and support.

Strong, supportive, and trusting relationships between educators and students are a crucial resource for promoting resilient school communities. The quality of trust between students and teachers was a distinctive feature of schools that mitigated the negative effects of proximity to homicide and a focus of the efforts that principals, educators, and school staff in these schools described in interviews. Investing in and bolstering the quality of relationships and relational trust between adults and students in schools represents a particularly important dimension of the work of fostering and supporting the resilience of students who experience adversity in their lives outside of school. Continuing to support school leaders and educators in developing and sustaining effective approaches to building empathy with their students is an important investment in expanding the work of schools to support students' mental health and wellbeing. Likewise, supporting the efforts of school leaders, educators, and students alike to ground the development of trust and relationship in ongoing explorations and appreciation of the complexity of racial, cultural, and gender identities appears particularly important to fostering those vital connections. The adoption and expansion of efforts to make classrooms and schools less punitive and more restorative, responsive spaces is also a key strategy for focusing on building connection and community above compliance.

Staff in schools that mitigated the negative effects of proximity to homicide actively worked to center the lived experiences and perspectives of their students. Educators in these schools talked at length about the core value of centering and responding to the lived experiences and perspectives of their students, including those students whose lives outside of school included significant adversity. Educators in these schools reported that they responded to students' experience with violence, racism, poverty, and the threat and impact of the COVID-19 pandemic with empathy and compassion, but also in many instances with a sense of responsibility for engaging students directly in making meaning of their lives within, as well as beyond, the classroom and the school. In addition, educators also talked extensively about efforts to engage students directly in efforts to create, sustain, and shape the communal life of a school in ongoing ways that supported students' own resilience and vitality. Their reflections on their practice often centered on the brilliance and creativity of the young people in front of them each day. Students' cultural values and traditions were critically important frames for making sense of their lived experiences, and their perspectives and desires were crucial resources, which educators in these schools described drawing on in fostering students' sense of themselves, their own identities and agency, and their resilience in the face of adversity, including but not limited to violence.

Schools that mitigated the negative effects of proximity to homicide did not develop out of just one initiative. Far from being the product of any single support structure, intervention, or practice, the insulating effects of these schools were the complex output of an intricate system of intentional, dynamic, and interconnected choices. The extent to which schools are protective, this report suggests, hinges on the ways in which educators make choices that center, engage with, and respond to the experiences, perspectives, and agency of students in empathetic, non-punitive, and asset-focused ways.

The MTSS logic offers an especially useful way to think about what this report reveals. Within the findings from this report, as well as in the work of other researchers, there is clear and ample evidence for the importance of effective tier 3 practices—individualized, often clinical intervention strategies—for meeting the acute needs of students who are most directly affected by significant adverse experiences, such as living in close proximity to homicide, in some cases multiple times in a given school year. Likewise, this report and the work of other researchers in Chicago and elsewhere underscore the value of effective tier 2 practices—targeted intervention strategies that focus on addressing the experiences and meeting the needs of small groups of students, such as the Becoming a Man (BAM) and Working on Womanhood (WOW) programs—in addressing student mental health and wellness in systematic, ongoing ways. And finally, the findings from this report both provide some concrete description of and underscore the importance of tier 1 practices—in the form of schools' efforts to provide all students in the school with a culturally-sustaining, asset-focused, and standards-aligned set of learning opportunities centered on their experiences, perspectives, and cultural wealth. In schools that mitigated the negative effects of proximity to homicide, this report suggests that these sorts of tier 1 learning opportunities functioned as an indispensable substrate upon which subsequent layers of more intensive, individualized intervention and support were built. Tier 1 practices aim to produce school environments in which students feel seen, supported, and engaged in meaningful work.

References

Anderson, C.M., & Borgmeier, C. (2010)
Tier II Interventions within the framework of school-wide positive behavior support: Essential features for design, implementation, and maintenance. *Behavior Analysis in Practice, 3*(1), 33-45.

Andriesen, P. (2023, October 12)
Chicago homicides in 2022 up 43 percent above pre-pandemic levels. *Illinois Policy.* Retrieved from https://www.illinoispolicy.org/chicago-homicides-in-2022-up-43-above-pre-pandemic-levels/

Bellis, M.D.D. (2001)
Developmental traumatology: The psychobiological development of maltreated children and its implications for research, treatment, and policy. *Development and Psychopathology, 13*(3), 539-564.

Bonanno, G.A. (2004)
Loss, trauma, and human resilience: Have we underestimated the human capacity to thrive after extremely adverse events? *American Psychologist, 59*(1), 20-28.

Bonanno, G.A., & Mancini, A.D. (2012)
Beyond resilience and PTSD: Mapping the heterogeneity of responses to potential trauma. *Psychological Trauma: Theory, Research, Practice, and Policy, 4,* 74-83.

Bowen, N., & Bowen, G. (1999)
Effects of crime and violence in neighborhoods and schools on the school behavior and performance of adolescents. *Journal of Adolescent Research, 14*(3), 319-342.

Boyle, C. (2020, July 12)
Young Chicagoans march against gun violence, remember those they lost: "I'm tired of seeing my friends in caskets." *Block Club Chicago.* Retrieved from https://blockclubchicago.org/2020/07/12/goodkids-madcity-activists-want-2-of-police-budget-to-be-reallocated-for-schools-violence-prevention-instead/

Bucci, M., Marques, S.S., Oh, D., & Harris, N.B. (2016)
Toxic stress in children and adolescents. *Advances in Pediatrics, 63*(1), 403-428.

Chicago Public Schools. (n.d.a.)
Multi-Tiered System of Supports (MTSS). Retrieved from https://www.cps.edu/services-and-supports/special-education/understanding-special-education/multi-tiered-system-of-supports/

Chicago Public Schools. (n.d.b.)
Stats and facts. Retrieved from https://www.cps.edu/about/stats-facts/

Christian-Brandt, A.S., Santacrose, D.E., & Barnett, M.L. (2020)
In the trauma-informed care trenches: Teacher compassion satisfaction, secondary traumatic stress, burnout, and intent to leave education within underserved elementary schools. *Child Abuse & Neglect, 110*(3), 104437.

City of Chicago. (n.d.)
Violence and victimization trends. Retrieved from https://www.chicago.gov/city/en/sites/vrd/home/violence-victimization.html

City of Chicago Data Portal. (2020)
Chicago data portal. Retrieved from https://data.cityofchicago.org/

Cooper, A. (2017)
The longitudinal effects of violence exposure on delinquency and academic outcomes for African-American youth. College of Science and Health Thesis and Dissertations, DePaul University, Chicago.

Creswell, J.W., & Clark, V.L.P. (2017)
Designing and conducting mixed methods research (3rd Ed.). Thousand Oaks, CA: Sage Publications.

Darling-Hammond, S., Fronius, T.A., Sutherland, H., Guckenburg, S., Petrosino, A., & Hurley, N. (2020)
Effectiveness of restorative justice in US K-12 Schools: A review of quantitative research. *Contemporary School Psychology, 24*(3), 295-308.

Delancy-Black, V., Covington, C., Ondersma, S., Nordstrom-Klee, B., Templin, T., Ager, J., Janisse, J., & Sokol, R. (2002)
Violence exposure, trauma, and IQ and/or Reading deficits among urban children. *American Medical Association, 156*(3), 280-285.

Dombo, E.A., & Sabatino, C.A. (2019)
The ten principles of trauma-informed services and application to school environments. Oxford, UK: Oxford Academic.

Domitrovich, C.E., Bradshaw, C.P., Poduska, J.M., Hoagwood, K., Buckley, J.A., Olin, S., Romanelli, L.H., Leaf, P.J., Greenberg, M.T., & Ialongo, N.S. (2008)
Maximizing the implementation quality of evidence-based preventive interventions in schools: A conceptual framework. *Advances in School Mental Health Promotion, 1*(3), 6-28.

Dunn, E.C., Nishimi, K., Powers, A., & Bradley, B. (2017)
Is developmental timing of trauma exposure associated with depressive and post-traumatic stress disorder symptoms in adulthood? *Journal of Psychiatric Research, 84,* 1191127.

Duplechain, R., Reigner, R., & Packard, A. (2008)
Striking differences: The impact of moderate and high trauma on reading achievement. *Reading Psychology, 29*(2), 117-136.

Eiraldi, R., McCurdy, B., Schwartz, B., Wolk, C.B., Abraham, M., Jawad, A.F., Nastasi, B.K., & Mautone, J.A. (2019)
Pilot study for the fidelity, acceptability, and effectiveness of a PBIS program plus mental health supports in under-resourced urban schools. *Psychology in the Schools, 56*(8), 1230-1245.

Essary, J.N., Barza, L., & Thurston, R.J. (2020)
Secondary traumatic stress among educators. *Kappa Delta Pi Record, 56*(3), 116-121.

Farmer, E.M.Z., Burns, B.J., Phillips, S.D., Angold, A., & Costello, E.J. (2003)
Pathways into and through mental health services for children and adolescents. *Psychiatric Services, 54*(1), 60-66.

Farmer, P. (2003)
Pathologies of power: Health, human rights, and the new war on the poor. Berkeley, CA: University of California Press.

Finkelhor, D., Turner, H., Shattuck, A., Hamby, S., & Kracke, K. (2015)
Children's exposure to violence, crime, and abuse: An update. Washington, DC: Office of Juvenile Justice and Delinquency Prevention.

Franke, H.A. (2014)
Toxic stress: Effects, prevention and treatment. *Children, 1*(3), 390-402.

Ginwright, S.A. (2010)
Black youth rising: Activism and radical healing in urban America. New York, NY: Teachers College Press.

Ginwright, S.A. (2015)
Radically healing Black lives: A love note to justice. *New Directions for Student Leadership, 2015*(148), 33-44.

Gordon, M.F., & Hart, H. (2022)
How strong principals succeed: Improving student achievement in high-poverty urban schools. *Journal of Educational Administration, 60*(3), 288-302.

Gorman-Smith, D., Henry, D., & Tolan, P. (2004)
Exposure to community violence and violence perpetration: The protective effects of family functioning. *Journal of Clinical Child & Adolescent Psychology, 33*(3), 439-449.

Gorman-Smith, D., & Tolan, P. (1998)
The role of exposure to community violence and developmental problems among inner-city youth. *Development and Psychopathology, 10*(1), 101-116.

Hardaway, C.R., Sterrett-Hong, E., Larkby, C.A., & Cornelius, M.D. (2016)
Family resources as protective factors for low-income youth exposed to community violence. *Journal of Youth and Adolescence, 45*(7), 1309-1322.

Henrich, C.C., Schwab-Stone, M., Fanti, K., Jones, S.M., & Ruchkin, V. (2004)
The association of community violence exposure with middle-school achievement: A prospective study. *Journal of Applied Developmental Psychology, 25*(3), 327-348.

Herrenkohl, T.I., Tajima, E.A., Whitney, S.D., & Huang, B. (2005)
Protection against antisocial behavior in children exposed to physically abusive discipline. *Journal of Adolescent Health, 36*(6), 457-465.

Huang, L.N. (2014)
SAMHSA's concept of trauma and guidance for a trauma-informed approach (HHS Publication Number (SMA) 14-4884). Rockville, MD: Substance Abuse and Mental Health Services Administration.

Jackson, C.K., Porter, S.C., Easton, J.Q., Blanchard, A., & Kiguel, S. (2020)
School effects on socioemotional development, school-based arrests, and educational attainment. *American Economic Review: Insights, 2*(4), 491-508.

Jocson, R.M., Alers-Rojas, F., Ceballo, R., & Arkin, M. (2020)
Religion and spirituality: Benefits for Latino adolescents exposed to community violence. *Youth & Society, 52*(3), 349-376.

Kittelman, A., McIntosh, K., & Hoselton, R. (2019)
Adoption of PBIS within school districts. *Journal of School Psychology, 76,* 159-167.

Koedel, C., Mihaly, K., & Rockoff, J.E. (2015)
Value-added modeling: A review. *Economics of Education Review, 47,* 180-195.

Li, M., Gao, T., Su, Y., Zhang, Y., Yang, G., D'Arcy, C., & Meng, X. (2022)
The timing effect of childhood maltreatment in depression: A systematic review and meta-analysis. *Trauma, Violence, and Abuse, 24*(4), 2560-2580.

Li, S.T., Nussbaum, K.M., & Richards, M.H. (2007)
Risk and protective factors for urban African-American youth. *American Journal of Community Psychology, 39* (1-2), 21-35.

Loftin, C., McDowall, D., Curtis, K., & Fetzer, M.D. (2015)
The accuracy of supplementary homicide report rates for large U.S. cities. *Homicide Studies, 19*(1), 6-27.

Lösel, F., & Farrington, D.P. (2012)
Direct protective and suffering protective factors in the development of youth violence. *American Journal of Preventive Medicine, 43*(2), S8-S23.

Loury, A. (2023, June 19)
Chicago remains the most segregated big city in America. WBEZ Chicago. Retrieved from https://www.wbez.org/stories/chicago-remains-the-most-segregated-big-city-in-america/2ec026b3-b11b-4c68-872b-3a1011b6f457?utm_medium=url_copy

Ludwig, J. (2023, March 27)
Jens Ludwig: Public safety inequality is growing in Chicago and across America. *Chicago Tribune.* Retrieved from https://www.chicagotribune.com/opinion/commentary/ct-opinion-public-safety-inequality-chicago-gun-violence-20230327-hpvtrnxx75gb5p7vvg5z4pch6q-story.html

Ludwig, K.A., & Warren, J.S. (2009)
Community violence, school-related protective factors, and psychosocial outcomes in urban youth. *Psychology in the Schools, 46*(10), 1061-1073.

Matthews, T., Dempsey, M., & Overstreet, S. (2009)
Effects of exposure to community violence on school functioning: The mediating role of posttraumatic stress symptoms. *Behaviour Research and Therapy, 47*(7), 586-591.

McCabe, K., Clark, R., & Barnett, D. (1999)
Family protective factors among urban African American youth. *Journal of Clinical Child Psychology, 28*(2), 137-150.

Mellin, E.A., Taylor, L., & Weist, M.D. (2014)
The expanded school mental health collaboration instrument [School Version]: Development and initial psychometrics. *School Mental Health, 6*(3), 151-162.

Moon, J., Williford, A., & Mendenhall, A. (2017)
Educators' perceptions of youth mental health: Implications for training and the promotion of mental health services in schools. *Children and Youth Services Review, 73*, 384-391.

Moradi, A.R., Doost, H.T, Taghavi, M.R., Yule, W., & Dalgleish, T. (1999)
Everyday memory deficits in children and adolescents with PTSD: Performance on the Rivermead Behavioural Memory Test. *The Journal of Child Psychology and Psychiatry and Allied Disciplines, 40*(3), 357-361.

Nygaard, M.A., Ormiston, H.E., Heck, O.C., Apgar, S., & Wood, M. (2023)
Educator perspectives on mental health supports at the primary level. *Early Childhood Education Journal, 51*(5), 851-861.

O'Donnell, D., Schwab-Stone, M., & Muyeed, A. (2002)
Multidimensional resilience in urban children exposed to community violence. *Child Development, 73*(4), 1265-1282.

Ormiston, H.E., Nygaard, M.A., Heck, O.C., Wood, M., Rodriguez, N., Maze, M., Asomani-Adem, A.A., Ingmire, K., Burgess, B., & Shriberg, D. (2021)
Educator perspectives on mental health resources and practices in their school. *Psychology in the Schools, 58*(11), 2148-2174.

Osborn, A.F. (1990)
Resilient children: A longitudinal study of high achieving socially disadvantaged children. *Early Child Development and Care, 62*(1), 23-47.

Osher, D., Guarino, K., Jones, W., & Schanfield, M. (2021)
Trauma-sensitive schools and social and emotional learning: An integration. Arlington, VA: American Institutes for Research.

Overstreet, S., & Braun, S. (1999)
A preliminary examination of the relationship between exposure to community violence and academic functioning. *School Psychology Quarterly, 14*, 380-396.

Ozer, E.J., Lavi, I., Douglas, L., & Wolf, J.P. (2017)
Protective factors for youth exposed to violence in their communities: A review of family, school, and community moderators. *Journal of Clinical Child & Adolescent Psychology, 46*(3), 353-378.

Ozer, E.J., & Weinstein, R.S. (2004)
Urban adolescents' exposure to community violence: The role of support, school safety, and social constraints in a school-based sample of boys and girls. *Journal of Clinical Child and Adolescent Psychology, 33*(3), 463-476.

Park-Higgerson, H.K., Perumean-Chaney, S.E., Bartolucci, A.A., Grimley, D.M., & Singh, K.P. (2008)
The evaluation of school-based violence prevention programs: A meta-analysis. *Journal of School Health, 78*(9), 465-479.

Parker, C., Scott, S., & Geddes, A. (2019)
Snowball sampling. Thousand Oaks, CA: Sage Research Methods Foundations.

Pavelka, S. (2013)
Practices and policies for implementing restorative justice within schools. *The Prevention Researcher, 20*(1), 15-18.

Peña, M. (2021, November 23)
After early hardships, this Chicago PE teacher relishes being a role model. *Chalkbeat Chicago.* Retrieved from https://chicago.chalkbeat.org/2021/11/23/22789396/chicago-public-schools-how-i-teach-physical-education-social-emotional-learning

Peña, M. (2022, May 10)
Chicago Public Schools partners with Lady Gaga foundation to tackle depression, mental health issues among students. *Chalkbeat Chicago.* Retrieved from https://chicago.chalkbeat.org/2022/5/10/23066091/chicago-public-schools-mental-health-resources-lady-gaga-please-stay-pandemic

Peña, M. (2022, December 9)
"Just as hard as last year": Inside a social worker's efforts to support a Chicago school. *Chalkbeat Chicago.* Retrieved from https://chicago.chalkbeat.org/2022/12/9/23500744/chicago-public-schools-social-worker-student-mental-health-covid-trauma-support-services

Pepper, J., Petrie, C., & Sullivan, S. (2010)
Measurement error in criminal justice data. In A.R. Piquero & D. Weisburd (Eds.), *Handbook of quantitative criminology* (pp. 353–374). New York, NY: Springer.

Pierre, C.L., Burnside, A., & Gaylord-Harden, N.K. (2020)
A longitudinal examination of community violence exposure, school belongingness, and mental health among African-American adolescent males. *School Mental Health, 12*(2), 388-399.

Porter, S., Jackson, C.K., Kiguel, S., & Easton, J.Q. (2023)
Investing in adolescents: High school climate and organ zational context shape student development and educational attainment. Chicago, IL: University of Chicago Consortium on School Research.

Raudenbush, S.W. (2004)
What are value-added models estimating and what does this imply for statistical practice? *Journal of Educational and Behavioral Statistics, 29*(1), 121-130.

Raviv, T., Smith, M., Hurwitz, L., Gill, T.L., Baker, S., Torres, S.A., Bowen, I. E., & Cicchetti, C. (2022)
Supporting school-community collaboration for the implementation of a multi-tiered school mental health program: *The Behavioral Health Team Model. Psychology in the Schools, 59*(6), 1239-1258.

Rowlands, D.W., & Love, H. (2022, April 21)
Mapping gun violence: A closer look at the intersection between place and gun homicides in four cities. *Brookings.* Retrieved from https://www.brookings.edu/2022/04/21/mapping-gun-violence-a-closer-look-at-the-intersection-between-place-and-gun-homicides-in-four-cities/

Rutter, M. (1985)
Resilience in the face of adversity: Protective factors and resistance to psychiatric disorder. *British Journal of Psychiatry, 147,* 598-611.

Sartain, L., Allensworth, E.M., Porter, S., Levenstein, R., Johnson, D.W., Huynh, M.H., Anderson, E., Mader, N., & Steinberg, M.P. (2015)
Suspending Chicago's students: Differences in discipline practices across schools. Chicago, IL: University of Chicago Consortium on Chicago School Research.

Sharkey, P. (2010)
The acute effect of local homicides on children's cognitive performance. *Proceedings of the National Academy of Sciences, 107*(26), 11733-11738.

Sharkey, P. (2018)
The long reach of violence: A broader perspective on data, theory, and evidence on the prevalence and consequences of exposure to violence. *Annual Review of Criminology, 1*(1), 85-102.

Sharkey, P., Schwartz, A.E., Ellen, I.G., & Lacoe, J. (2014)
High stakes in the classroom, high stakes on the street: The effects of community violence on student's standardized test performance. *Sociological Science, 1,* 199-220.

Sharkey, P., Tirado-Strayer, N., Papachristos, A.V., & Raver, C.C. (2012)
The effect of local violence on children's attention and impulse control. *American Journal of Public Health, 102*(12), 2287-2293.

Shonkoff, J.P., Garner, A.S., The Committee on Psychosocial Aspects of Child and Family Health, C. on E.C., Siegel, B.S., Dobbins, M.I., Earls, M.F., Garner, A.S., McGuinn, L., Pascoe, J., & Wood, D.L. (2012)
The Lifelong effects of early childhood adversity and toxic stress. *Pediatrics, 129*(1), e232–e246.

Starkey, L., Aber, J.L., & Crossman, A. (2019)
Risk or resource: Does school climate moderate the influence of community violence on children's social-emotional development in the Democratic Republic of Congo? *Developmental Science, 22*(5), e12845.

Steinberg, M.P., Allensworth, E., & Johnson, D.W. (2011)
Student and teacher safety in Chicago Public Schools: The roles of community context and school social organization. Chicago, IL: University of Chicago Consortium on Chicago School Research.

Stephan, S.H., Weist, M., Kataoka, S., Adelsheim, S., & Mills, C. (2007)
Transformation of children's mental health services: The role of school mental health. *Psychiatric Services, 58*(10), 1330-1338.

Stieber, D. (2023, March 13)
Teaching through the trauma of student loss—EdSurge News. *EdSurge.* Retrieved from https://www.edsurge.com/news/2023-03-13-teaching-through-the-trauma-of-student-loss

Stouthamer-Loeber, M., Loeber, R., Farrington, D.P., Zhang, Q., van Kammen, W., & Maguin, E. (1993)
The double edge of protective and risk factors for delinquency: Interrelations and developmental patterns. *Development and Psychopathology, 5*(4), 683-701.

Taylor, L., & Adelman, H.S. (2000)
Toward ending the marginalization and fragmentation of mental health in schools. *Journal of School Health, 70*(5), 210-215.

Thomas, M.S., Crosby, S., & Vanderhaar, J. (2019)
Trauma-informed practices in schools across two decades: An interdisciplinary review of research. *Review of Research in Education, 43*(1), 422-452.

Thurlow, M.L., Ghere, G., Lazarus, S.S., & Liu, K.K. (2020)
MTSS for all: Including students with the most significant cognitive disabilities. Minneapolis, MN: National Center on Educational Outcomes and the TIES Center.

Turner, K. (2021, September 3)
Youth leadership program empowers Bronzeville students to put ideas into action for community change. *South Side Weekly.* Retrieved from https://southsideweekly.com/youth-leadership-program-empowers-bronzeville-students/

U.S. Department of Education. (2023)
Characteristics of public school teachers (Condition of Education). Washington, DC: National Center for Education Statistics, Institute of Education Sciences. Retrieved from https://nces.ed.gov/programs/coe/indicator/clr/public-school-teachers

University of Illinois at Chicago. (2023)
Law enforcement epidemiology project. Retrieved from https://policeepi.uic.edu/

Walker Burke, C. (2021, May 14)
What do Chicago students say they most need? Counselors, school board seats, therapy dogs. *Chalkbeat Chicago.* Retrieved from https://chicago.chalkbeat.org/2021/5/14/22436635/what-do-chicago-students-say-they-most-need-counselors-mental-health-school-board-seats-therapy-dogs

Walker, H.M., & Horner, R.H. (1996)
Integrated approaches to preventing antisocial behavior patterns among school-age children and youth. *Journal of Emotional & Behavioral Disorders, 4*(4), 194-209.

Wyman, P.A., Cowen, E.L., Work, W.C., & Parker, G.R. (1991)
Developmental and family milieu correlates of resilience in urban children who have experienced major life stress. *American Journal of Community Psychology, 19*(03), 405-426.

Yule, K., Houston, J., & Grych, J. (2019)
Resilience in children exposed to violence: A meta-analysis of protective factors across ecological contexts. *Clinical Child and Family Psychology Review, 22*(3), 406-431.

Appendix A

Student and Teacher Survey-Based Measures of School Climate

This appendix includes additional information regarding the survey measures used in our analyses to identify and describe key characteristics of the climate and organization of schools that were more successful at mitigating the negative effects of proximity to homicide. The survey data used in these analyses were from 2010–11 to 2018–19. The numbers of survey respondents and response rates are summarized in **Table A.1**. The measures used are summarized and grouped in **Table A.2**, by *5Essentials* Survey measure, and labeled according to whether they were taken from the student or teacher survey (see p.53).

The measures included in the analysis were selected by the research team in a three-stage process that combined review of previous research with close analysis of qualitative data (i.e., interviews with educators and school staff in the three high schools included in this study). In the first stage of this process, the research team reviewed previous research on the effects of proximity to violence on child and adolescent development and academic performance, focusing specifically on research that attempted to identify protective factors that prior studies appeared to suggest might mitigate negative impacts on students development or academic trajectories.[91] That research is also reviewed in the introduction of this report.

A substantial body of existing literature on protective factors focused on individual characteristics associated with resilience to adverse experience, including studies that explored the role of particular personality characteristics, temperament, dimensions of self-perception, aspects of spirituality, and biological (genetic or hormonal) characteristics.[92] Findings from previous research strongly suggested that the quality of relationships between young people and adults was likely to be associated with school protectiveness for students who lived in close geographic proximity to homicide. **This research suggested that survey measures which measured the quality of relationships between young people and adults in schools were likely to be associated with school protectiveness.**

TABLE A.1

Survey respondents and response rates by year

Survey year (Spring)	Number of schools surveyed	Student response rate	Teacher response rate	Number of students who responded	Number of teachers who responded	Total students	Total teachers
2011	680	74.2%	48.6%	146,429	11,798	197,268	24,263
2012	677	73.5%	65.4%	143,803	15,823	195,544	24,211
2013	695	77.0%	81.1%	149,309	19,441	193,835	23,981
2014	658	78.8%	80.9%	149,156	18,844	189,229	23,299
2015	679	79.5%	80.7%	152,724	19,908	192,032	24,661
2016	676	83.0%	83.2%	157,628	24,145	189,940	29,020
2017	665	82.2%	80.9%	153,102	23,185	186,337	28,646
2018	661	81.4%	79.9%	149,334	22,691	183,526	28,400
2019	659	81.4%	78.5%	148,713	22,563	182,632	28,743
Average		**79.00%**	**75.47%**				

91 Lösel & Farrington (2012).

92 Jocson, Alers-Rojas, Ceballo, & Arkin (2020); Lösel & Farrington (2012); Ozer et al. (2017); Yule, Houston, & Grych (2019).

In addition to individual-level factors, the research team also identified a body of research that explored the contextual factors or environmental circumstances associated with more positive outcomes for youth living in close proximity to violence. In turn, much of that literature focused on characteristics of families and home environments, including findings that suggested that parenting approaches which emphasized *"intensive supervision, high persistence of discipline, low physical punishment, and strong involvement of the child in the family's activities"* had direct protective effects for children.[93] Broadly, parenting practices that emphasize close supervision of children, a high degree of parental involvement, and a warm and accepting family environment have been characterized as protective for young people.[94] **This research suggested again that survey measures that measured the quality of relationships between young people and adults in schools, and that specifically focused on aspects of adult behavior like close supervision, strong but non-punitive discipline, and consistent involvement in the lives of young people, were likely to be associated with school protectiveness.**

The research team also reviewed literature exploring the protectiveness of peer relationships for young people living in proximity to homicide. That literature treated the element of peer support as supplementary to other (usually family-related) spheres of influence. When combined with, for example, family-based protective factors, youth involvement with peer groups can be conceived of as having a pro-social, potentially protective impact on young people.[95] **This research suggested that survey measures which measured the extent and quality of peer relationships might be associated with school protectiveness.**

The research team also reviewed previous research that strongly suggested that living in neighborhoods with high levels of social cohesion can serve as a protective factor for young people. Some research suggests that neighborhood social cohesion may be reflective of more extensive forms of informal social control that may be embedded within neighborhoods through neighbors, such as neighborhood level associations and other adults that can provide parents with support in parenting and supervising youth activity.[96] Some evidence also suggests that students' perception of the extent of social cohesion characteristic of their school climates, including the positivity and predictability of adult behavior, may also be protective.[97] **This research again underscored the likely association between survey measures of the quality of relationships between young people and adults, as well as the quality of coordination and cohesion characteristic of adults' work in schools with school protectiveness.**

A final, albeit relatively limited, body of research reviewed by the research team focused specifically on the potential protective role of schools in the lives of young people living in close geographic proximity to homicide. The studies reviewed suggested that high levels of prior academic achievement may function as protective for students.[98] Relatedly, measures of students' motivation in school, their desire to complete college, their perceived bonding or connection to school, and their experiences of clear, consistent, and positive school climate were all characterized as protective factors in prior studies.[99] Students' perception of their schools as safe, including lower levels of student misbehavior (e.g., arguing, fighting, etc.) and of their peers as engaged in more positive, consistent academic behaviors (e.g., on-task, on-time, etc.), were also characterized as protective dimensions of school climate.[100] Students' perceptions of their teachers as supportive, invested, and holding high expectations and positive regard for students were also found to be potentially protective for students exposed to violence.[101] **These findings underscored the importance of not only the relational contexts that students experience within schools, but also suggest that measures of students' perceptions of their schools and classrooms—and particularly,**

---

93 Lösel & Farrington (2012).
94 Gorman-Smith & Tolan (1998); Hardaway et al. (2016); Lösel & Farrington (2012); McCabe et al. (1999).
95 Ozer et al. (2017).
96 Cooper (2017); Lösel & Farrington (2012); Yule et al. (2019).
97 Starkey et al. (2019).
98 Lösel & Farrington (2012).
99 Herrenkohl, Tajima, Whitney, & Huang (2005).
100 Ludwig & Warren (2009); O'Donnell et al. (2002); Starkey et al. (2019).
101 Ludwig & Warren (2009).

of their peers behaviors and the responsiveness and supportiveness of adults in those environments—are likely to be associated with school protectiveness.

The close review of the existing research literature provided a first set of guideposts for the research team in identifying and selecting measures from the student and teacher surveys for inclusion in our analysis.

A second, parallel stage of the work of identifying survey measures for inclusion in our analysis included close thematic analysis of the qualitative data collected in the three high schools identified and included in this study. See Chapter 1 for a full description of the selection of those three high schools. While researchers reviewed evidence from prior research, the team also looked closely at the themes that emerged from the interviews conducted with educators and school staff in those three high schools, focusing specifically on the dimensions of school organization and climate that educators' experiences and perspectives seemed to suggest were closely connected to their work with young people living in close geographic proximity to homicide. **The qualitative findings from this study, including the importance of strong, supportive relationships between young people and adults, the experience of academically-focused, student-centered, and culturally responsive classroom contexts, and the presence of strong, coordinated, and coherent systems of adult supervision, monitoring, and support, provided a second set of guideposts for the research team in identifying measures from the student and teacher survey for inclusion in our analysis of the characteristics of schools that were more successful at mitigating the negative effects of proximity to homicide.**

The third and final stage of the process of identifying student and teacher survey measures for inclusion in our analysis of the characteristics of schools that were more successful at mitigating the negative effects of proximity to homicide was the crosscheck the results of the first (literature review) and second (qualitative analysis) stages against one another systematically, in order to identify where there was common and/or compelling evidence across both that argued for the inclusion of one or another student and/or teacher survey measure. From that cross-checking of the findings from both stages, the research team identified the measures presented in **Table A.2** for inclusion in the analysis.

TABLE A.2

Survey measures and descriptions by survey and by essential

Measure	Description	Survey	Essential
Academic Press	Asks students' views of their teachers' efforts to push students to higher levels of academic performance. Students also report on teachers' expectations of student effort and participation. High levels that most teachers press all students toward academic achievement.	Student	Ambitious Instruction
Teacher-Teacher Trust	Measures the extent to which teachers feel they have mutual respect for one another, for those who lead school improvement efforts, and for those who are experts at their craft. Also asks teachers whether they feel comfortable discussing feelings and worries, as well as trust their colleagues. High levels of teacher-teacher trust indicate that teachers trust and respect each other.	Teacher	Collaborative Teachers
Collective Responsibility	Measures teacher assessments of the strength of their shared commitment to improve so that all students learn. Questions ask teachers how many colleagues feel responsible for students' academic and social development, set high standards for professional practice, and take responsibility for school improvement. High levels of collective responsibility indicate that the teachers have a strong sense of shared responsibility.	Teacher	Collaborative Teachers
School Commitment	Reflects the degree to which teachers felt loyal and committed to the school. Questions ask teachers whether they look forward to going to work, would rather work somewhere else, and whether they would recommend the school to parents. High levels of school commitment indicate teachers are deeply committed to the school.	Teacher	Collaborative Teachers
Teacher-Principal Trust	Reflects the degree to which teachers feel their principal respects and supports them. Questions ask teachers whether the principal looks out for their welfare, has confidence in the expertise, is an effective manager, and whether teachers respect the principal as an educator. High levels of teacher-principal trust indicate the teachers share deep mutual trust and respect with the principal.	Teacher	Effective Leaders
Teacher Influence	Reflects the degree to which teachers are involved in school decision-making. Questions ask teachers about their influence in the selection of instructional materials, setting of school policy, in-service program planning, spending of discretionary funds, and hiring of professional staff. High levels of teacher influence indicate that teachers have a high degree of influence across a broad range of issues within the school.	Teacher	Effective Leaders
Peer Support for Academic Work	Reveals whether prevailing norms among students support academic work. Students reported whether their friends try hard to get good grades, do their homework regularly, pay attention in class and follow school rules. In schools with high scores, students experience support from their peers for academic work. As a result, student learning is more likely.	Student	Supportive Environment
Academic Personalism	Gauges whether students perceive that their classroom teachers give them individual attention and show personal concern for them. Students were asked if their teachers know and care about them, notice if they are having trouble in class, and are willing to help with academic and personal problems. A high score here means students experience strong personal support from school staff.	Student	Supportive Environment
Student-Teacher Trust	Reveals the quality of relationships between students and teachers. Students were asked whether they believe teachers can be trusted, care about them, keep their promises, and listen to students' ideas, and if they feel safe and comfortable with their teachers. In high-scoring schools, there is a high level of care and communication between students and teachers.	Student	Supportive Environment
Course Clarity	Captures students' views about what they need to do to succeed in the target class, their learning from feedback, and how helpful the homework and class work are.	Student	N/A; supplemental measure
Academic Engagement	Academic Engagement examines student interest and engagement in learning. Students responded to items regarding whether they are interested in their class and the topics studied. They also reported whether they work hard to do their best. A high score means greater individual engagement in learning.	Student	N/A; supplemental measure
Importance of High School for the Future	Students were asked questions about their attitudes regarding the importance of high school. Students' beliefs about the value of high school have been linked to how well they perform in college.	Student	N/A; supplemental measure
School Connectedness	Asks whether or not students feel included in their school's community.	Student	N/A; supplemental measure

Appendix B

Distribution of School-Average Change in Outcomes

As shown in Chapter 4, there were differences between schools in how much student outcomes changed with proximity to homicide, even after adjusting for school and student characteristics. This appendix shows the distribution of those school-average impacts by grade category for each outcome-grade category combination where that difference was statistically significant across students.

Test scores

Figure B.1 shows the distribution of school-average change in test scores with proximity to homicide for high school students. We excluded schools with fewer than 100 students in the grade category or with fewer than 30 students in either the "lives in proximity to homicide" group or the "does not live in proximity to homicide" group; the estimates for schools below these thresholds are statistically imprecise.

FIGURE B.1

High school test scores declined with proximity to homicide in some schools but not in other schools

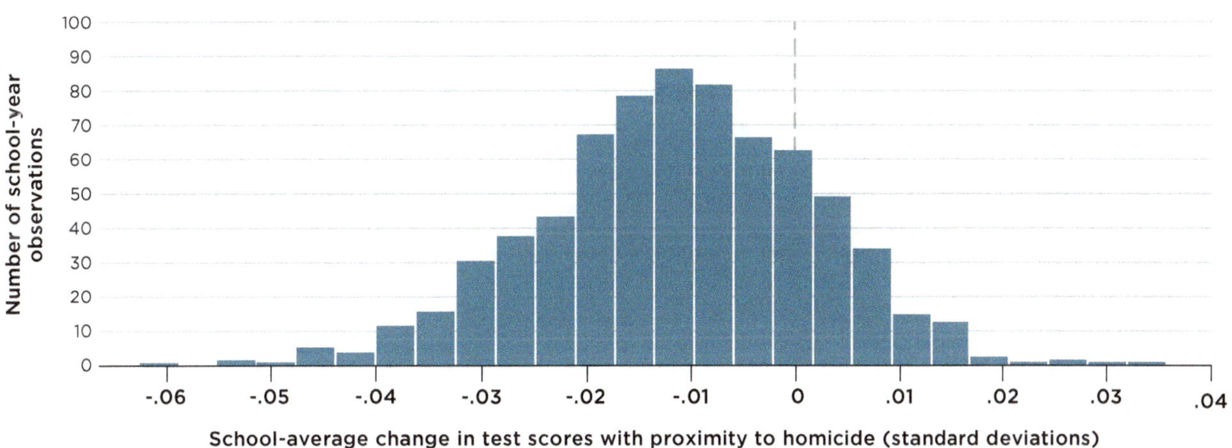

Note: The change in test score with proximity to homicide is estimated separately for each school in each year. This figure plots the distribution of school-by-year estimates for high schools. Estimates are adjusted for school characteristics (e.g., baseline outcomes, percent of students living in proximity to homicide, in special education, eligible for free/reduced-price lunch, ever retained, and attending zoned school, as well as school racial composition, and average neighborhood social status and concentration of poverty).

GPA

Figure B.2 shows the distribution of school-average change in GPA with proximity to homicide for high school students. Student GPA had a statistically significant decline for grades 1-2; however, we did not estimate school-specific measures at that grade level for most schools due to sample restrictions. We excluded schools with fewer than 100 students in the grade category or with fewer than 30 students in either the "lives in proximity to homicide" group or the "does not live in proximity to homicide" group; the estimates for schools below these thresholds are statistically imprecise. School-specific estimates were excluded for many schools because early elementary students were more likely to be missing GPA data than other data and this category was based on two grades rather than three or four.

FIGURE B.2

High school GPA declined with proximity to homicide in some schools but not in other schools

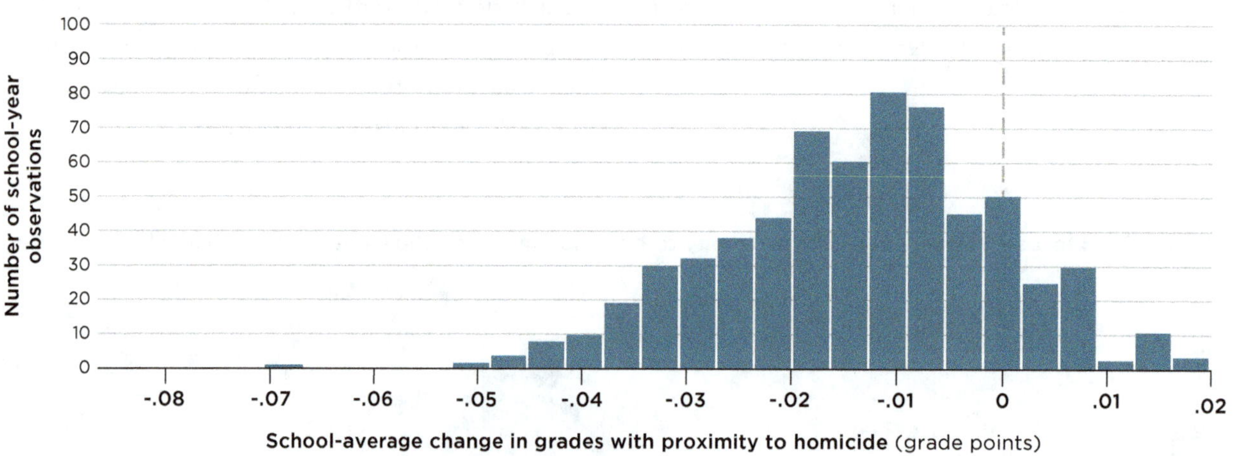

Note: The change in grades with proximity to homicide is estimated separately for each school in each year. This figure plots the distribution of school-by-year estimates for high schools. Estimates are adjusted for school characteristics (e.g., baseline outcomes, percent of students living in proximity to homicide, in special education, eligible for free/reduced-price lunch, ever retained, and attending zoned school, as well as school racial composition, and average neighborhood social status and concentration of poverty)..

Attendance

Figures B.3-B.6 show the distribution of school-average change in attendance (days attended) with proximity to homicide for each of the grade groups. We excluded schools with fewer than 100 students in the grade category or with fewer than 30 students in either the "lives in proximity to homicide" group or the "does not live in proximity to homicide" group; the estimates for schools below these thresholds are statistically imprecise. The sample is smaller for grades 1-2 because fewer schools had enough students in those grades to produce a reliable estimate.

FIGURE B.3

Grade 1-2 attendance declined with proximity to homicide in some schools but not in other schools

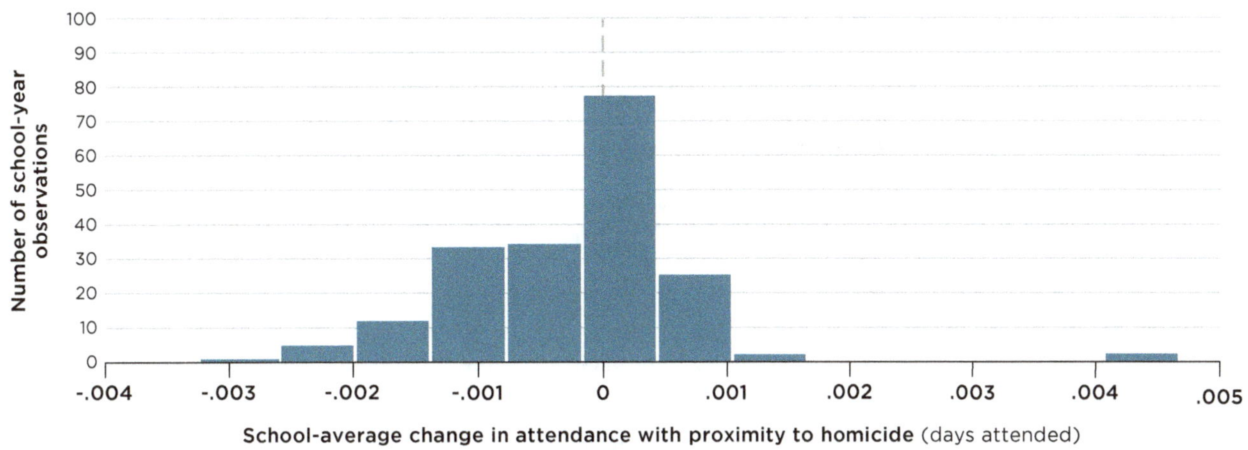

Note: The change in attendance with proximity to homicide is estimated separately for each school in each year. Estimates are adjusted for school characteristics (e.g., baseline outcomes, percent of students living in proximity to homicide, in special education, eligible for free/reduced-price lunch, ever retained, and attending zoned school, as well as school racial composition, and average neighborhood social status and concentration of poverty). There were fewer schools in this figure than for other grades because fewer schools had enough students in these grades to produce a reliable estimate.

FIGURE B.4

Grades 3-5 attendance declined with proximity to homicide in some schools but not in other schools

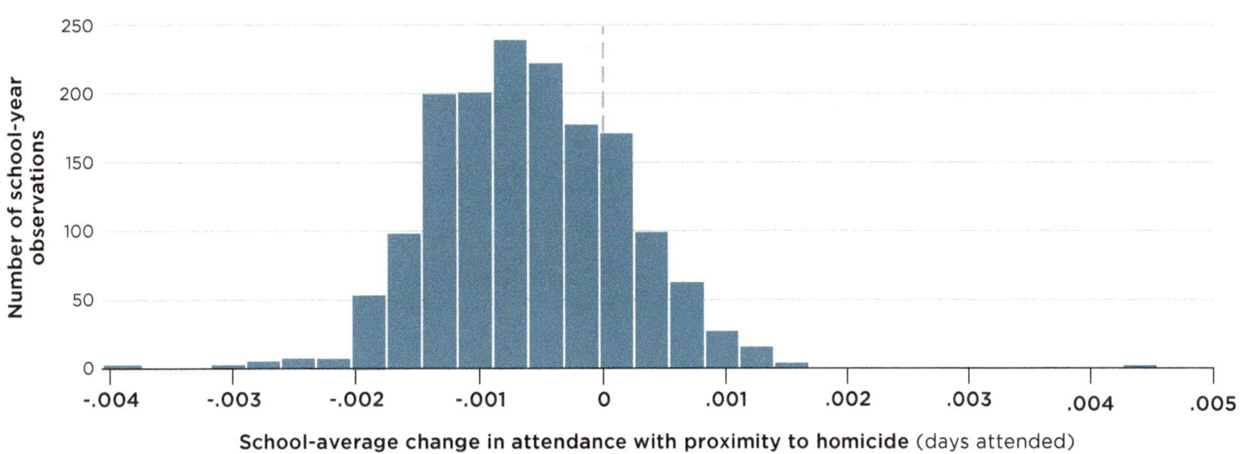

Note: The change in attendance with proximity to homicide is estimated separately for each school in each year. Estimates are adjusted for school characteristics (e.g., baseline outcomes, percent of students living in proximity to homicide, in special education, eligible for free/reduced-price lunch, ever retained, and attending zoned school, as well as school racial composition, and average neighborhood social status and concentration of poverty).

FIGURE B.5

Grades 6-8 attendance declined with proximity to homicide in some schools but not in other schools

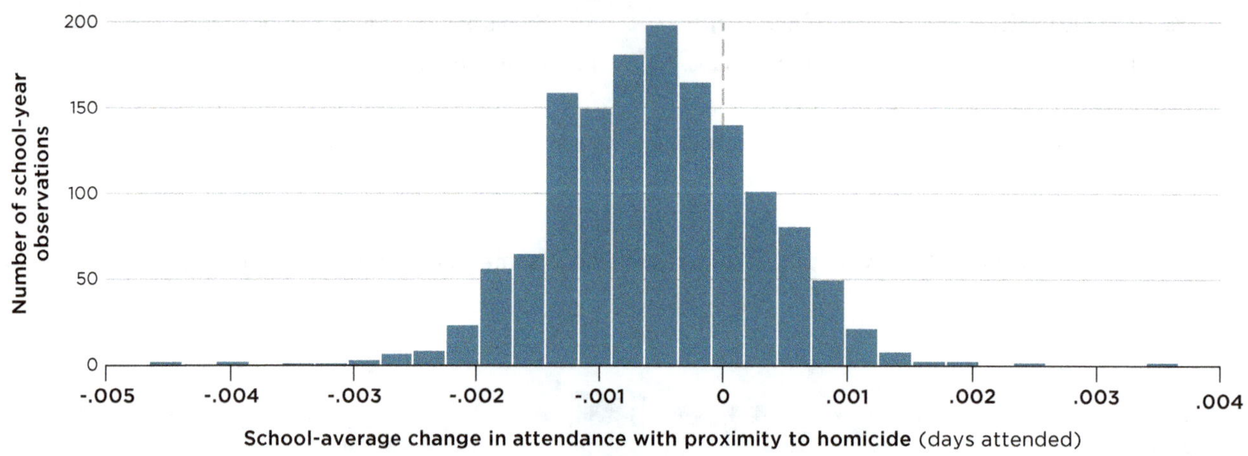

Note: The change in attendance with proximity to homicide is estimated separately for each school in each year. Estimates are adjusted for school characteristics (e.g., baseline outcomes, percent of students living in proximity to homicide, in special education, eligible for free/reduced-price lunch, ever retained, and attending zoned school, as well as school racial composition, and average neighborhood social status and concentration of poverty).

FIGURE B.6

High school attendance declined with proximity to homicide in some schools but not in other schools

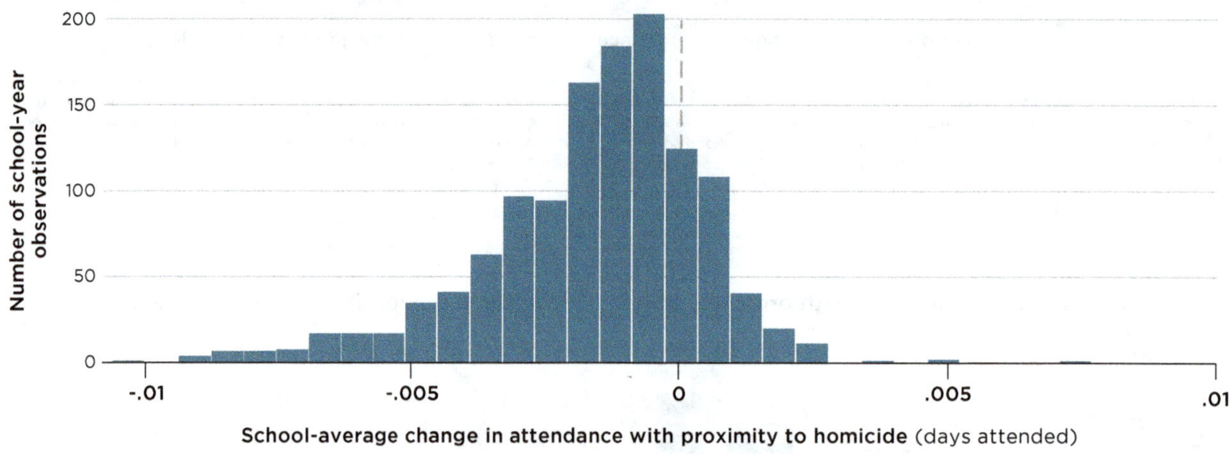

Note: The change in attendance with proximity to homicide is estimated separately for each school in each year. Estimates are adjusted for school characteristics (e.g., baseline outcomes, percent of students living in proximity to homicide, in special education, eligible for free/reduced-price lunch, ever retained, and attending zoned school, as well as school racial composition, and average neighborhood social status and concentration of poverty).

Behavioral infractions

Figures B.7 and B.8 show the distribution of school-average change in behavioral infractions with proximity to homicide for high school students. We excluded schools with fewer than 100 students in the grade category or with fewer than 30 students in either the "lives in proximity to homicide" group or the "does not live in proximity to homicide" group; the estimates for schools below these thresholds are statistically imprecise.

The shape of the distribution of school-specific estimates looks different for behavioral infractions. It appears skewed, with the peak of the distribution to the left of zero and a long tail to the right. It is possible that at some schools, the likelihood of a behavioral infraction could decline in years of proximity to homicide while at other schools it increases. These differences may be due to differences in the overall risk of behavioral infraction between schools, due to differences in educator practice, differences in student behaviors themselves, or from some other process.

FIGURE B.7

Grade 1-2 behavioral infractions increased with proximity to homicide

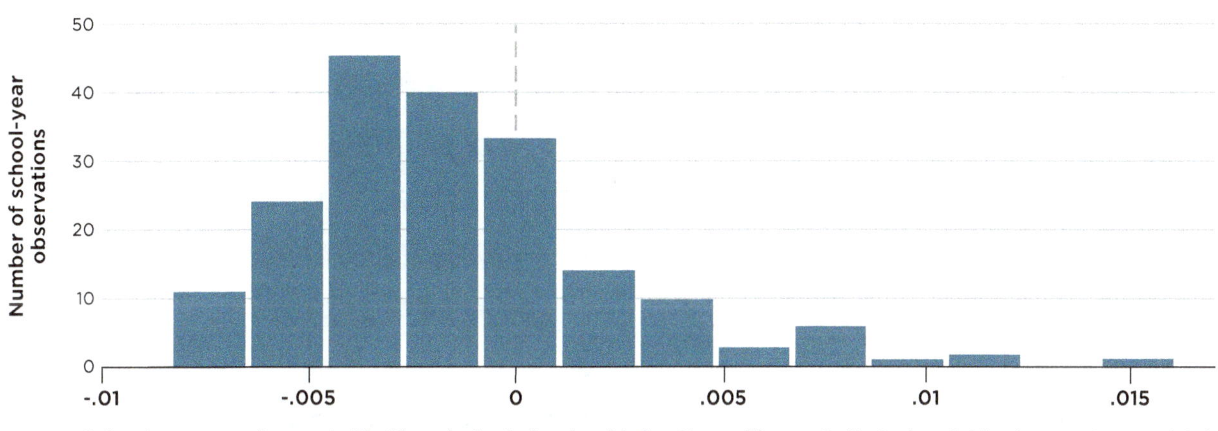

Note: The change in the likelihood that a student had a behavioral infraction with proximity to homicide is estimated separately for each school in each year. Estimates are adjusted for school characteristics (e.g., baseline outcomes, percent of students living in proximity to homicide, in special education, eligible for free/reduced-price lunch, ever retained, and attending zoned school, as well as school racial composition, and average neighborhood social status and concentration of poverty). There were fewer schools in this figure than for other grades because fewer schools had enough students in these grades to produce a reliable estimate.

FIGURE B.8

High school behavioral infractions increased with proximity to homicide in some schools

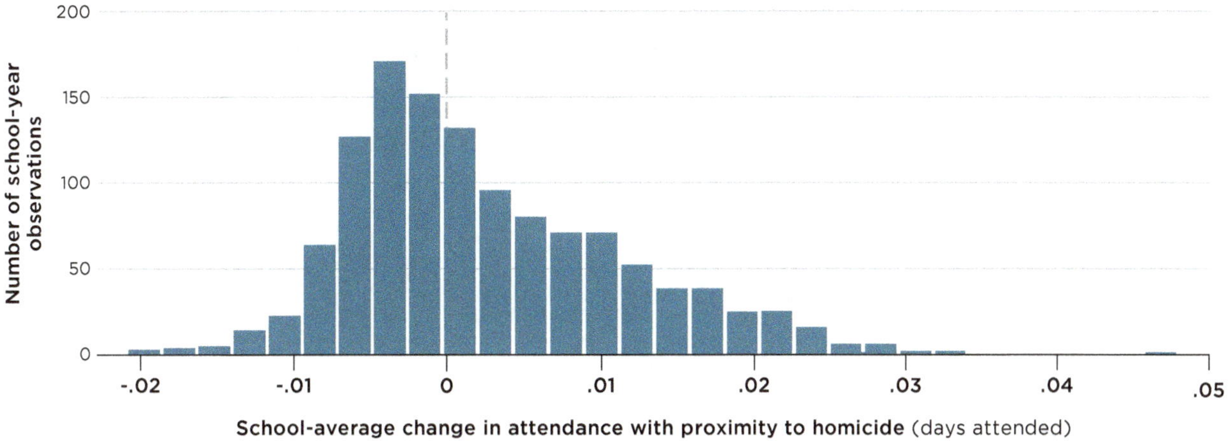

Note: TThe change in the likelihood that a student had a behavioral infraction with proximity to homicide is estimated separately for each school in each year. Estimates are adjusted for school characteristics (e.g., baseline outcomes, percent of students living in proximity to homicide, in special education, eligible for free/reduced-price lunch, ever retained, and attending zoned school, as well as school racial composition, and average neighborhood social status and concentration of poverty).

Appendix C

Distribution of School Characteristics

There were no systematic differences in student characteristics between schools did and did not mitigate negative effects of living in close proximity to homicide and other schools, as shown in **Figures C.1–C.6**. Although there were some apparent minor differences in distributions, those differences were not consistently present across test scores, attendance, GPAs, and behavioral infractions, and did not consistently emerge across school characteristics.

FIGURE C.1

The distribution of school-level proximity to homicide was similar across all schools

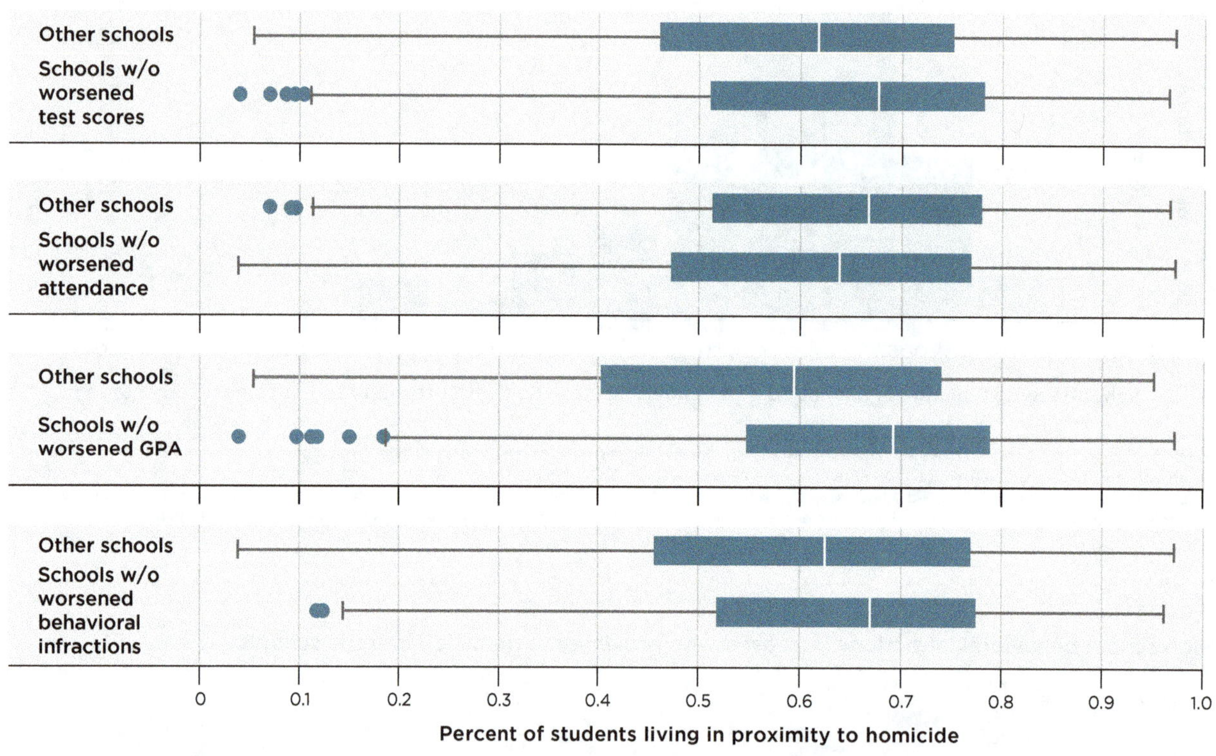

Note: For each of the four outcomes (test scores, attendance, GPA, and behavioral infractions), schools were split into those that did and did not mitigate negative effects of living in proximity to homicide. The horizontal bars represent the distribution of the schools in the two groups on percent of students living in proximity to homicide. The vertical line at the middle of each bar is the median value and the horizontal whiskers display the edges of the distribution. The dots are schools that were statistical outliers within the distribution.

FIGURE C.2

The distribution of school-average neighborhood social status score was similar across all schools

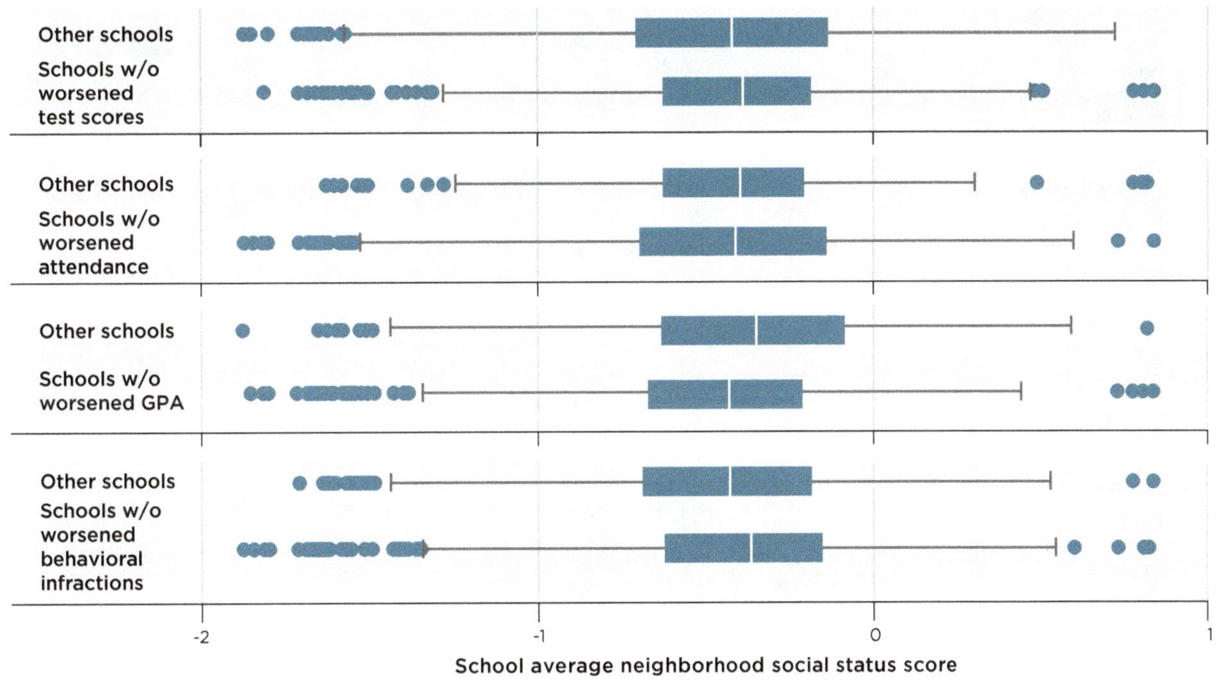

Note: For each of the four outcomes (test scores, attendance, GPA, and behavioral infractions), schools were split into those that did and did not mitigate negative effects of living in proximity to homicide. The horizontal bars represent the distribution of the schools in the two groups on school average neighborhood social status score. The vertical line at the middle of each bar is the median value and the horizontal whiskers display the edges of the distribution. The dots are schools that were statistical outliers within the distribution. Social status score was calculated for each student's census block group from data on the mean level of education of adults and the percentage of employed persons who work as managers or professionals.

ɪURE C.3

ə distribution of school-average concentrated neighborhood poverty score was similar across all schools

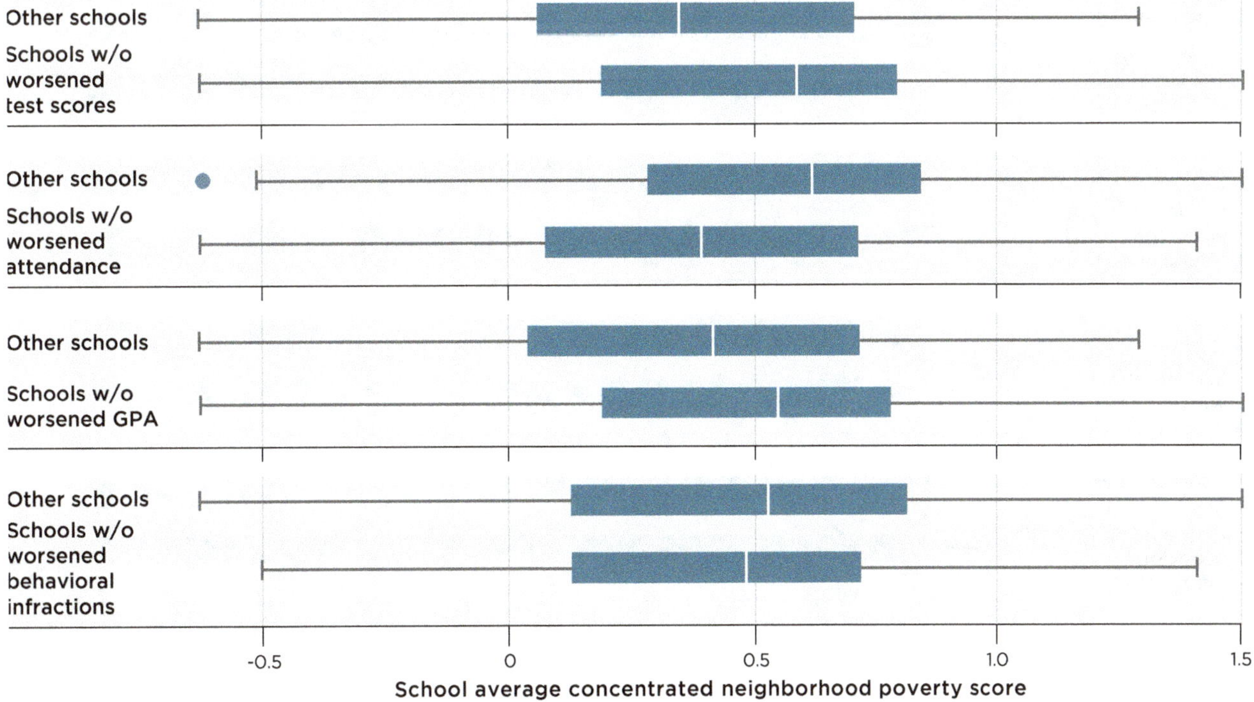

ə: For each of the four outcomes (test scores, attendance, GPA, and behavioral infractions), schools were split into those that did and did not mitigate negative ɔts of living in proximity to homicide. The horizontal bars represent the distribution of the schools in the two groups on school average concentrated neighborhood ərty score. The vertical line at the middle of each bar is the median value and the horizontal whiskers display the edges of the distribution. The dots are schools were statistical outliers within the distribution. Concentrated neighborhood poverty was calculated for each student's census block group as a combination of the

FIGURE C.4

The distribution of school-level free/reduced-price lunch eligibility was similar across all schools

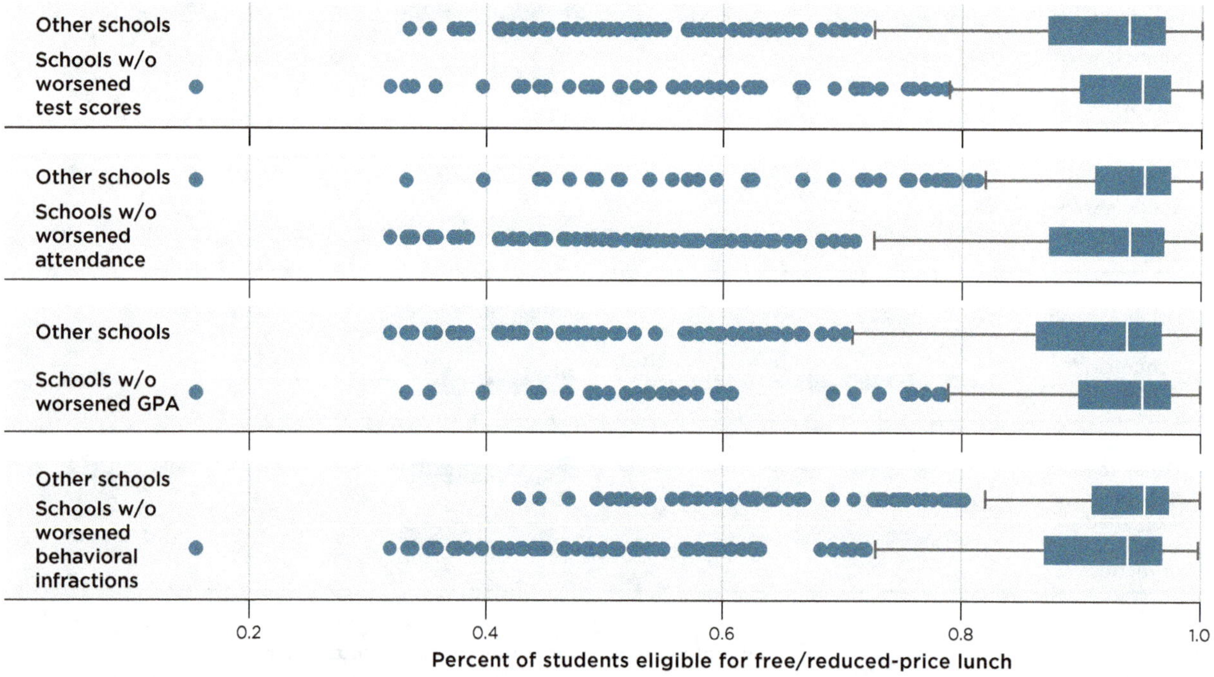

Note: For each of the four outcomes (test scores, attendance, GPA, and behavioral infractions), schools were split into those that did and did not mitigate negative effects of living in proximity to homicide. The horizontal bars represent the distribution of the schools in the two groups on percent of students eligible for free/reduced-price lunch. The vertical line at the middle of each bar is the median value and the horizontal whiskers display the edges of the distribution. The dots are schools that were statistical outliers within the distribution.

FIGURE C.5

The distribution of percent of Black students within total school enrollment was similar across all schools

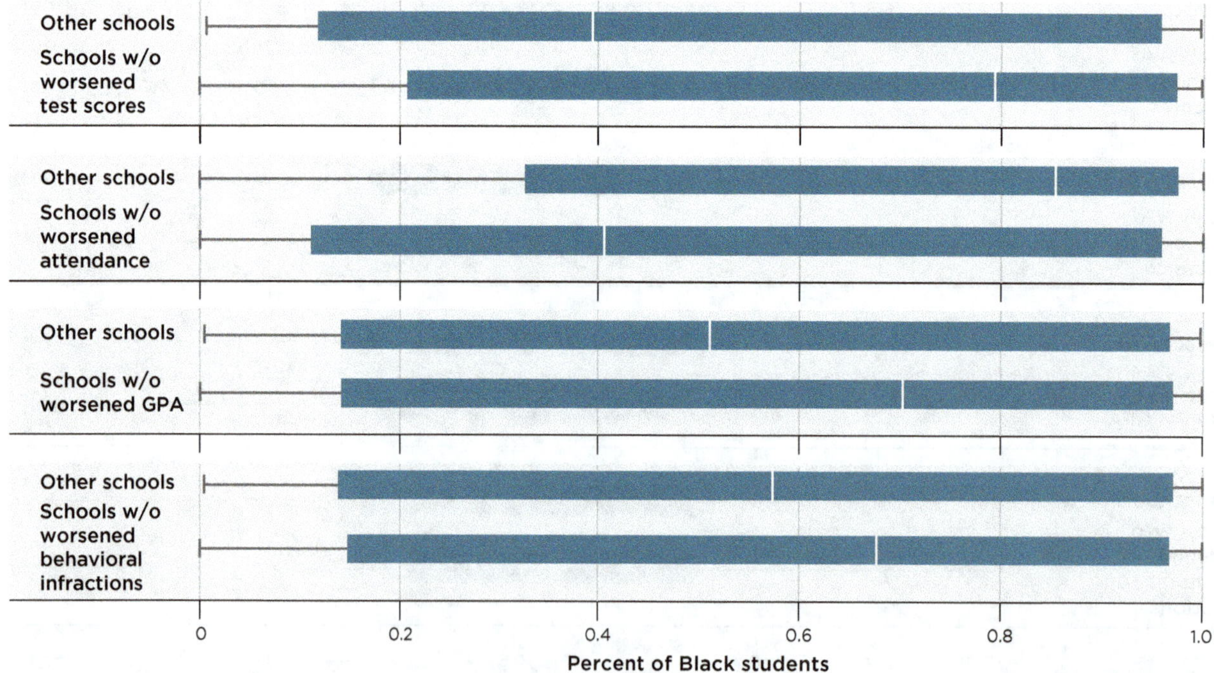

Note: For each of the four outcomes (test scores, attendance, GPA, and behavioral infractions), schools were split into those that did and did not mitigate negative effects of living in proximity to homicide. The horizontal bars represent the distribution of the schools in the two groups on percent of Black students. The vertical line at the middle of each bar is the median value and the horizontal whiskers display the edges of the distribution. The dots are schools that were statistical outliers within the distribution.

FIGURE C.6

The distribution of percent of Latinx students within total school enrollment was similar across all schools

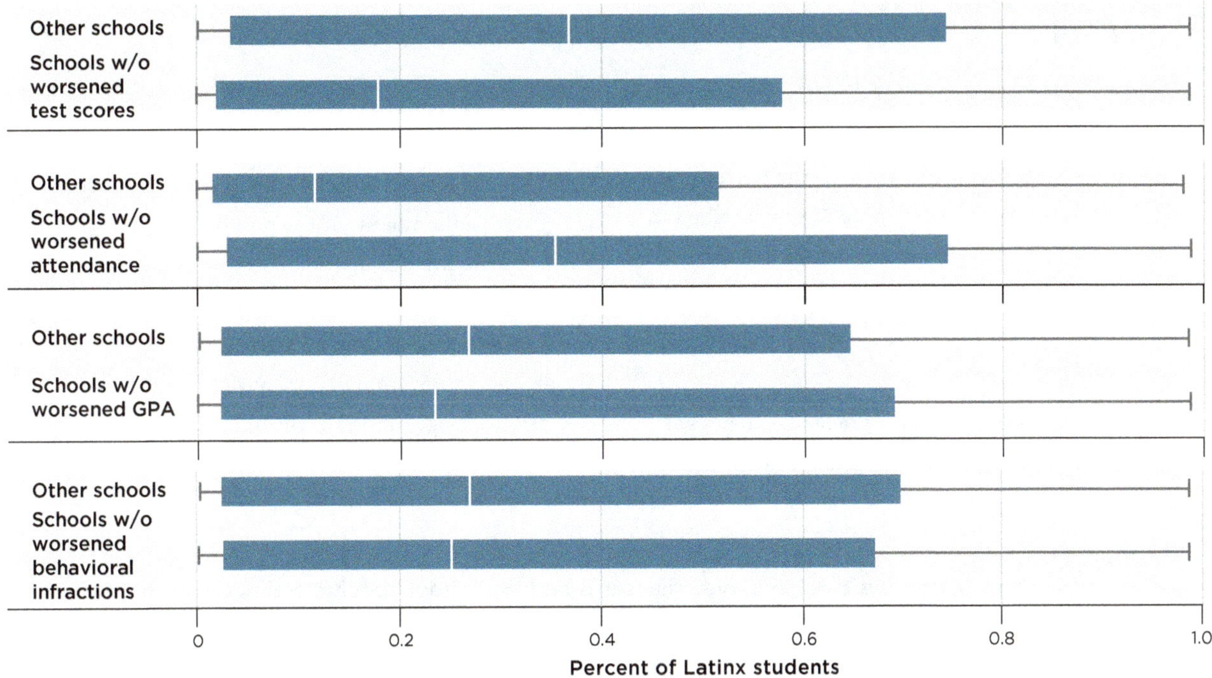

Note: For each of the four outcomes (test scores, attendance, GPA, and behavioral infractions), schools were split into those that did and did not mitigate negative effects of living in proximity to homicide. The horizontal bars represent the distribution of the schools in the two groups on percent of Latinx students. The vertical line at the middle of each bar is the median value and the horizontal whiskers display the edges of the distribution. The dots are schools that were statistical outliers within the distribution.

Appendix D

Associations between School-Specific Effects and Survey Measures

The tables in this appendix provide the regression coefficients used to construct **Table 3.** As described in Chapter 1, these coefficients are calculated via ordinary least squares (OLS) regression:

$$\Delta\hat{Y}_{st} = \alpha_0 + \alpha_1 M_{st} + \alpha_2 Exp_{st} + \varepsilon_{st}$$

In this regression, the school-grade category-year change in student outcomes with proximity to homicide ($\Delta\hat{Y}_{st}$) is associated with the noted survey measure (M_{st}), with adjustment for the percent of students who lived in proximity to homicide in that year (Exp_{st}). The values in **Tables D.1 and D.3** are the estimated coefficient on the survey measure, α_1. They denote the change in $\Delta\hat{Y}_{st}$ that occurs with a one standard deviation change in the survey measure.

TABLE D.1

Association between *5Essentials* teacher survey measures and the school-specific estimates of the shift in student outcomes with proximity to homicide

	GPA	Test scores	Infractions	Suspensions	Attendance
Classroom Disruptions	*-.0059**** *(.0010)*	*-.0019** *(.0008)*	*.0034**** *(.0005)*	*.0033**** *(.0005)*	*-.0008**** *(.0000)*
Teacher Collaboration	.0015 (.0010)	.0010 (.0006)	.0001 (.0004)	.0002 (.0003)	.0001 (.0001)
Collective Responsibility	.0051*** (.0008)	.0010 (.0006)	-.0019*** (.0003)	-.0017*** (.0003)	.0001 (.0001)
Teacher Influence	.0035*** (.0008)	-.0008 (.0006)	-.0002 (.0004)	.0001 (.0004)	.0001 (.0001)
Instructional Leadership	.0018* (.0008)	.0003 (.0006)	-.0003 (.0004)	-.00001 (.0004)	-.00001 (.0001)
Program Coherence	.0040*** (.0007)	.0008 (.0006)	-.0008* (.0003)	-.0009* (.0003)	.0001* (.0001)
Reflective Dialogue	.0028** (.0009)	.0014* (.0006)	.0001 (.0004)	.0003 (.0004)	-.0001 (.0001)
School Commitment	0054*** (.0008)	-0001 (.0006)	-.0016*** (.0004)	-.0018*** (.0004)	0003*** (.0001)
Teacher-Principal Trust	.0023** (.0007)	.0005 (.0005)	-.0013*** (.0003)	-.0015*** (.0004)	.0001 (.0001)
Teacher-Teacher Trust	.0045*** (.0007)	.0005 (.0006)	-.0008* (.0003)	-.0011** (.0003)	.0001 (.0001)
Disorder and Crime	*-.0055**** *(.0007)*	*-.0004* *(.0007)*	*.0034**** *(.0004)*	*.0034**** *(.0004)*	*-.0006**** *(.0000)*

Note: *Italics* indicate the natural direction of the survey measure is reversed—signifying that the implication of a positive or negative association is opposite for the classroom disruptions and disorder/crime measures. Test scores are measured in standard deviation units. GPA is measured in grade points. Attendance is measured in number of days attended. Suspensions are measured in percentage point likelihood of receiving a suspension. Survey measures are in standard deviation units.

TABLE D.2

Association between *5Essentials* student survey measures and the school-specific estimates of the shift in student outcomes with proximity to homicide

	GPA	Test scores	Infractions	Suspensions	Attendance
Peer Support for Academic Work	.0007 (.0011)	.0041*** (.0008)	-.0009 (.0007)	-.0004 (.0006)	.0003** (.0001)
Course Clarity	.0032** (.0010)	.0006 (.0006)	-.0015*** (.0004)	-.0012** (.0004)	.0003*** (.0001)
Emotional Health	.0017* (.0008)	-.0008 (.0007)	-.0007 (.0004)	-.0015** (.0004)	.00024** (.00009)
Academic Engagement	.0047*** (.0011)	.0004 (.0007)	-.0002 (.0004)	-.0004 (.0004)	.0001 (.0001)
Classroom Behavior	.0065*** (.0007)	-.0001 (.0007)	-.0036*** (.0004)	-.0036*** (.0004)	.0005*** (.0001)
Classroom Professionalism	.0043*** (.0011)	.0003 (.0006)	-.0008* (.0004)	-.0004 (.0003)	.0001 (.0001)
Academic Press	.0013 (.0009)	-.0001 (.0007)	-.0022*** (.0004)	-.0018*** (.0004)	-.0004*** (.0001)
School Connectedness	.0030*** (.0008)	-.0012 (.0008)	-.0020*** (.0004)	-.0017*** (.0004)	.0002** (.0001)
Classroom Rigor	.0036*** (.0008)	-.0004 (.0007)	-.0022*** (.0004)	-.0020*** (.0004)	.0004*** (.0001)
Safety	.0055*** (.0009)	.0005 (.0008)	-.0035*** (.0005)	-.0032*** (.0005)	.0004*** (.0001)
School-level Academic Press	.0044*** (.0009)	.0002 (.0006)	-.0027*** (.0004)	-.0024*** (.0004)	.0003*** (.0001)
School Safety	*-.0045**** *(.0008)*	*.0004* *(.0008)*	*.0031**** *(.0004)*	*.0032**** *(.0004)*	*-.0002*** *(.0001)*
Rigorous Study Habits	.0007 (.0008)	-.0014 (.0008)	-.0018*** (.0005)	-.0018*** (.0005)	.0001 (.0001)
Student-Teacher Trust	.0080*** (.0010)	-.0004 (.0008)	-.0019*** (.0004)	-.0020*** (.0005)	.0002** (.0001)

Note: *Italics* indicate the natural direction of the survey measure is reversed—signifying that the implication of a positive or negative association is opposite for the classroom disruptions and disorder/crime measures. Test scores are measured in standard deviation units. GPA is measured in grade points. Attendance is measured in number of days attended. Suspensions are measured in percentage point likelihood of receiving a suspension. Survey measures are in standard deviation units.

ABOUT THE AUTHORS

DAVID W. JOHNSON is a Research Assistant Professor at the Center for Childhood Resilience in the Pritzker Department of Psychiatry and Behavioral Health at Lurie Children's Hospital. At the time this research was conducted, David was a Senior Research Analyst at the UChicago Consortium, where he served in various capacities for 15 years. David's research focuses broadly on how school and classroom contexts affect the mental and behavioral health and wellness of young people, as well as their academic achievement and attainment. David's research explores the contexts and experiences that contribute to how both children and adults learn. Prior projects include efforts to describe and understand the noncognitive factors that shape students' academic success, as well as the creation of a developmental framework for understanding young adult success inside and beyond school. David has also been closely involved in the planning and facilitation of a national network of school support organizations and school districts aimed at creating more equitable learning environments for historically marginalized and oppressed children and communities. His past and current work reflect a thoroughgoing commitment to building the capacity of educators to create developmentally rich learning experiences for all children, particularly across lines of racial, class, and cultural difference. David is a former Washington, DC Public Schools teacher and holds master's degrees in social service administration and divinity, and a doctorate in social service administration from the University of Chicago Crown Family School of Social Work, Practice, and Policy.

REBECCA HINZE-PIFER is an Assistant Professor in Education Policy, Organization, and Leadership at the University of Illinois Urbana-Champaign. Rebecca's research focuses on school-based approaches to reducing social inequality, with particular focus on programs and practices influencing adolescent socioemotional development. Her work includes randomized field experiments of school-based programs and quasi-experimental studies using school administrative data to understand the impacts of school policies. Rebecca has published and presented on a range of related topics, including school discipline, teacher classroom management practices, and student responses to community violence. Rebecca was a public school teacher for seven years before earning her master's degree in public policy from George Washington University and her PhD in public policy from the University of Chicago.

DAVID ORTA is a sociologist from Chicago whose research centers on race, education, and inequality, focusing on trans-formational practice and policy. His previous work has been published in the *Journal of Hispanic Higher Education, Sociological Compass,* and *Social Sciences.* He holds a PhD in sociology from Texas A&M University and is currently a Senior Research Analyst at the UChicago Consortium.

SAMANTHA GUZ is a community social worker and writer living in Chicago. She is currently a doctoral candidate at the University of Chicago, studying direct practice at the nexus of the public education, non-profit, and criminal legal systems. She is a fellow at the National Institutes of Health and a Mansueto Institute Urban Doctoral Fellow. Her research has been funded by the William T. Grant Foundation, the Center for Health Administration Studies, and the Center for the Study of Race, Politics, and Culture. She received her master's degree in social work from the University of Texas at Austin and her bachelor's degree in psychology and sociology from Texas A&M University.

UCHICAGO Consortium on School Research

www.ingramcontent.com/pod-product-compliance
Lightning Source LLC
LaVergne TN
LVHW081254100826
845148LV00009B/1218

9780981460420